PRACTICAL LANGUAGE TEACHING
Editors: Marion Geddes and Gill Sturtridge

No. 10
Teaching Vocabulary

PRACTICAL LANGUAGE TEACHING
Editors: Marion Geddes and Gill Sturtridge

Teaching Vocabulary

MICHAEL J. WALLACE

HEINEMANN EDUCATIONAL BOOKS

Heinemann International
A division of Heinemann Educational Books Ltd
Halley Court, Jordan Hill, Oxford OX2 8EJ

OXFORD LONDON EDINBURGH
MELBOURNE SYDNEY AUCKLAND
SINGAPORE MADRID IBADAN
NAIROBI GABORONE HARARE
KINGSTON PORTSMOUTH (NH)

 British Library Cataloguing in Publication Data

Wallace, Michael J.
  Teaching vocabulary.—(Practical language
  teachings; no. 10)
  1. English language—Vocabulary—Study and
  teaching—Foreign students
  I. Title   II. Series
  428′.2   PE1128

ISBN 0 435 28974 8

Set in 10 on 12 Times by Castlefield Press, Northampton
and printed and bound in Great Britain by
Biddles Ltd, Guildford and King's Lynn

For Pat and Nancy

Acknowledgements

I should like to thank my editors, Marion Geddes and Gill Sturtridge, for initiating this project, and their much-appreciated friendship and encouragement in this as in other matters. I owe a debt of gratitude to Kathleen McGeorge, without whose efficient and willing secretarial assistance the writing of this book would have been a much more tedious task. Thanks also, as always, to my wife Eileen for her loyal support.

Note to the Reader

At the end of this book you will find some suggestions for further reading and also for activity/discussion. Even if you are working on your own, you will probably find it useful to work through (or think about) some of the suggestions for activity/discussion near the end of the book. In the text itself, nearly all the exercises and activities can be self-corrected by using the answer keys provided. For greater convenience, a special answer key will be found at the end of the book for the example exercises given in Chapters 5 and 6.

Contents

1 Learning a Foreign Language and Vocabulary

It has often been remarked how strange it is that comparatively little has been written on the teaching and learning of foreign language vocabulary, because there is a sense in which learning a foreign language is basically a matter of learning the vocabulary of that language. Not being able to find the words you need to express yourself is the most frustrating experience in speaking another language.

Of course vocabulary is not the whole story: the system of language (its 'grammar' or 'structure') is also important: how the plural is formed, how past tense is signified, and so on. Nevertheless, it is possible to have a good knowledge of how the system of a language works and yet not be able to communicate in it; whereas if we have the vocabulary we need it is usually possible to communicate, after a fashion.

This book is concerned with the most effective ways of teaching this vital aspect of language. Before going on to look at some basic background issues in vocabulary learning, we perhaps ought to begin by looking at some of the things which can go wrong when someone tries to learn the vocabulary from another language.

Some of the symptoms of bad vocabulary learning and/or teaching are:

1 Inability to retrieve vocabulary that has been taught
This is the most basic kind of vocabulary fault. The student has been exposed to a vocabulary item at some stage, but cannot bring it to mind when he needs it. In this situation, either communication breaks down altogether or else the student has to use some 'repair strategy', such as expressing his meaning in a different way.

2   *Use of vocabulary inappropriate to the given situation*

Here the student knows *a* word which has the particular meaning required, but somehow doesn't fit into the language situation in which he is operating. To take an obvious example: normally, *right* (hand side) and *left* (hand side) are perfectly acceptable ways of indicating direction, but on board a ship, there are situations where these terms would sound strange, the terms *port* (for left) and *starboard* (for right) being more appropriate. Similarly the progress of a ship is measured in *knots* (rather than *miles* or *kilometres*), and depth below sea-level sometimes in *fathoms* (rather than *feet* or *metres*); front and back become *fore* and *aft*; a *kitchen* becomes a *galley*; and so on. These examples (where a word that is correct in one situation is not correct in another, although it has the same kind of significance) could be paralleled in many other situations.

3   *Use of vocabulary at the wrong level of formality*

This is rather similar to the previous symptom – it also has to do with inappropriate use of language. The words we choose have to relate to the formality of the situation in which we are speaking, and the relationship between the speakers. Thus we go from the very formal, 'Be seated, ladies and gentlemen!', to the command 'Sit!' (which a teacher might give to a class), to the informal 'Have a seat', to the colloquial, joking expression 'Take a pew!'. *Pew* is, strictly speaking, the type of long, wooden seat found in a church: the meaning is sometimes humorously extended to any kind of chair. The effect of the expression here depends on the formal associations of pew (a seat in a church) with its use in an informal situation.

In learning a foreign language there is a tendency to use the more formal language found in textbooks in normal conversational situations, with results that sound strange to the native speaker. The reverse can also happen where a learner picks up a slang or colloquial expression and uses it inappropriately.

ꞏ4   *Possessing the wrong kind of vocabulary for one's needs*

What we have said previously leads naturally on to the problem of the kind of vocabulary that is appropriate to the needs of the learner. If the learner is going to be involved only in face-to-face contact with native speakers, then what he needs is the conversational language for those situations: it will not be much help to him to have a large reading vocabulary of words he can hardly pronounce. On the other hand, if the learner, as far as can be known, is going to be spending the rest of his life in his own country and needs English only for reading books in his area of specialism, then an extensive reading vocabulary may be precisely what is required: hours spent on conversational practice may be time wasted.

Also, of course, the area of study is important. Someone who is studying medicine in English needs to know English medical words and expressions. If at some stage he is going to be talking to native-speaker patients, then some knowledge of colloquial terms that occur in doctor–patient discussions may also be necessary; and so on.

5   *Using vocabulary in an unidiomatic way*

Even when a student has the right kind of vocabulary, he may use it in an unidiomatic way. We could take as an actual example the following extract from a brochure advertising a sea-cruise:

> The schedules take into account the wishes of those of you who use maritime transport both as a means of communication and rest and it goes without saying that you can have such rest in no else corner of our planet.

Obvious deviations from normal English idiom are: the use of *else* for *other*; the use of the phrase *'no else corner of our planet'* which is too 'elevated' for the topic; and, generally, the uneasy mixture of formal and informal language.

6   *Using vocabulary in a meaningless way*

This is the fault which John Bright has called 'verbalism'. He wittily uses the example of the 'Giky Martables'. Bright took a biology textbook and substituted a nonsense word for every word in the text that was outside the *General Service List* (this word-list will be discussed later in the present chapter: see p. 15). Part of the passage he uses runs like this (the nonsense words are in italics):

It must be admitted, however, that there is an occasional *pum-tumfence* of a diseased condition in wild animals, and we wish to call attention to a remarkable condition which seems like a *giky martable*. Let us return to the *retites*. In the huge societies of some of them there are guests or pets, which are not merely *briscerated* but fed and *yented*, the *spintowrow* being, in most cases, a *talable* or *spiskant exboration* – a *sunury* to the hosts.

As Bright points out, it is possible to ask a learner intermediate-level questions about this passage and get answers from him or her, in this way:

What does the remarkable condition which the writer calls attention to seem like? (It seems like a *giky martable*.)
What happens to the *retites*? (They are *briscerated*, fed and *yented*.)
What is the *spintowrow*, in most cases? (It's a *talabale* or *spiskant exboration*.)

The point being made here is that the learner does not have to be able to understand the question to be able to answer it in an apparently satisfactory way. The grammatical and contextual clues in the passage are enough to give the framework for his answer. The learner does not even have to understand his own answer: he is merely lifting phrases from the text.

The effect is that the student is *using* the target language, but he or she is not *learning* it, since no connection has been made between the vocabulary and meaning. This can all too easily happen in the question-and-answer routines of a second-language or foreign-language classroom.

7   *Incorrect use of a dictionary*

Some students are not aware of the most efficient way to use a dictionary. Others go to the other extreme and are over-conscious of the importance of checking individual words. Whenever they come across a new word in a passage, they will immediately stop and not proceed until they have checked it up in a dictionary. This can kill all interest and even interfere with comprehension because the reader is so concerned with the individual words that he is less aware of the context which gives them meaning. It also results in very slow and inefficient reading. Some learners, even in conversation, will stop to check up their bilingual dictionary for the word they need, instead of perhaps finding another way to express it or enlisting the help of the native speaker they may be talking to.

8   *Use of incorrect grammatical form, spelling, pronunciation, or stress*
These issues will be discussed below, p. 23–26.

The above is a list of some of the more obvious things that can go wrong in learning vocabulary. It will be clear that learning vocabulary is something more than memorizing lists of words. In the next chapter we shall look more closely at the positive aspects of learning and teaching vocabulary, as opposed to the things that can go wrong. But first let us look at some basic elements in considering vocabulary.

VOCABULARY: BASIC ELEMENTS

The linguistic study of vocabulary ('lexis') can lead us on to the discussion of all sorts of fascinating topics, some of which have only marginal relevance to language teaching. Nevertheless, it seems sensible to look at a few basic elements in the study of lexis which have obvious teaching implications, if only in making useful distinctions, and establishing some useful relationships.

FORM AND MEANING: WORDS AND LEXICAL ITEMS

Look at these sentences:

(1)   Jack was sitting on the bank of the river, fishing.
(2)   I am going to the bank to cash a cheque.

Is *bank* in sentence (1) the same word as *bank* in sentence (2)?

Obviously in one way it is the same word: it looks the same, it has the same *form*. But equally obviously, the word *bank* has a very different *meaning* in sentence (1) from the meaning of *bank* in sentence (2). Some people would make the distinction by saying that they are the same *word* because they have the same form, but they are different *lexical items* because they have different meanings. It is the context of the sentence which shows which meaning of *bank* is being used. Now look at this sentence:

I'm not going to put up with this kind of treatment any longer.

All the words in this sentence link with one another and help to make up the sense of the sentence, but three words in particular (put up with) are firmly linked together: they operate as a unit, and have one meaning (roughly, 'tolerate' or 'endure'). So here we have three *words* which form one *lexical item*. (*Put up with* is an example of a particular kind of idiom called a multi-word verb: these will be discussed in more detail in Chapter 8). The concept of lexical item as one kind of unit of meaning is a useful one to the teacher, as it helps to make clear what it is that is being taught. It reveals one reason why a 'difficult' word like *helicopter* which has only one meaning may be easier to teach than a 'simple' word like *head* which may be in fact several different lexical items (a hat on my head, at the head [= top] of the page, the head [= boss] of the business, to head [= lead] an expedition, etc.).

WORD-LISTS

It is this kind of consideration which makes the matter of word-counts and word-lists sometimes ambiguous. We see for example that a certain book has been written 'within a vocabulary of 2000 words'. Does this mean 2000 *forms* or 2000 *meanings* (i.e. 2000 lexical items)? Very often the list is a list of forms (i.e. words without meanings being differentiated) which in teaching terms means that the book may give rise to more problems in understanding than one might at first think since, obviously, the student may know the meaning of a word in one context but not in another.

One of the most famous word-lists in English is *Basic English*, devised by C. K. Ogden and I. A. Richards. These writers showed that almost anything in English could be expressed by using only 850 words. This would seem to simplify the learning of English considerably, but is it really as helpful as it seems? Among the 850 words are such words as *go*, *get*, *of*, *to*, etc., each of which has literally dozens of meanings, so that in terms of *lexical items* the learning task is much more formidable than the number 850 might suggest.

Furthermore, the use of 'simple' words (i.e. forms) may cause more problems for the learner than they prevent. The words *put*, *up*, and *with* are all in the Basic English list. If we take a sentence like:

I shall not tolerate this!

we have to consider whether it is really making it easier for the learner to express it as:

I shall not put up with this!

As we have seen above, the meaning of *put up with* as a unit has little in common with the meaning of these words in their most common senses. It may therefore be that the longer, more 'difficult' word is easier for the learner to understand!

GENERAL SERVICE LIST

One of the best known lists is *The General Service List of English Words* edited and compiled by Michael West and published by Longman. This list is based on a very large sample of some five million words, from which the 2000 most common words were extracted. One of the strengths of this list is that it takes into account not only words, but also lexical items, since different meanings of the same word are listed, and also idiomatic phrases containing the word in question. So we discover from this list that, in the count of 5 million words, the word *body* appeared an estimated 1699 times; 40

per cent of the times it appeared was in the sense of 'physical organism' (e.g. 'body and soul'); 26 per cent in the sense of 'a group' (e.g. 'Went in a body to the Town Hall'); 10 per cent in the sense of 'corpse'; 8 per cent in the sense of 'mass' (e.g. 'A falling body moves at the rate of ...'); 7 per cent in the sense of 'trunk' or 'main part' (e.g. 'Draw a body and add head, arms and legs'); some less frequent meanings are also listed. The frequency of idioms and phrases are also listed where they have occurred in the sample and are related to the 2000 words chosen for the list. *COBUILD*

Other, much more up-to-date word-lists have been drawn up, one of the most famous being based on a sample of over one million words assembled at Brown University in the United States during the years 1963-4 (for details, see Further Reading). This list contains over 50,000 words arranged in order of frequency. It also shows how they are spread over 15 categories, which include religion, general fiction, etc. However, the main concern of all the lists we have been discussing is *how frequently* words occur. Is frequency the best criterion for choosing vocabulary to be taught?

There is a common-sense argument which tells us that it is sensible to teach very common words (like *big* and *small*) before we teach more unusual words like *gigantic* or *microscopic*. Yet frequency need not be the only criterion for vocabulary selection.

AVAILABILITY

There is also the criterion of availability (sometimes the French term *disponibilité* is used). In certain learning situations, rather unusual words may be of the greatest usefulness. For example, in the General Service List the word *chalk* has a very low frequency (only 78 occurrences in 5 million words) and *blackboard* is not listed at all. In a classroom situation, however, both these words may be very useful indeed because they name things which the learner can see and touch, and which the teacher can use in his or her teaching. They have high *availability* in that particular situation. So words may be learned or taught because they are seen to be of special relevance to particular situations in which the learner finds himself, or might find himself.

ESP VOCABULARY

This is an especially important consideration in the matter of English for Special Purposes (ESP). A word may be of relatively rare occurrence in the total use of English, but absolutely essential for, say, a biochemist who wishes to read learned articles on his specialism which happens to be written in English. So we come to the idea of special kinds of vocabulary (words or expressions) which are relevant to special interests or fields of knowledge. There is another aspect to this, however, and it is the question of *learnability*. Let us take the example of a Spanish-speaking scientist (male) who is doing a course in ESP for (perhaps) chemistry. One of the words that he will probably have to know is *carbon*. However, he should find this very easy to learn since, as a scientist, he will already be very familiar with the concept being referred to (in this case one of the common elements). All he has to learn therefore is the label to attach to a concept that he is already familiar with. Moreover (and this is especially true of the physical sciences) the English word may be a *cognate* of the word which the scientist already knows (i.e. derived from the same root: in the example we have given, the Spanish word is *carbono*, the French *carbone* and so on). It may be also a loan-word from English perhaps, or an English loan-word from the learner's language.

In situations where English is taught as a *second* language, the learner has a more difficult task. In the case, for example, of a Kenyan schoolgirl studying chemistry at secondary level, she has the problem of not only learning the label *carbon*, but also understanding the concept which goes with it: and in that case her situation is somewhat similar to a British or American schoolgirl at the same level.

The serious problem for the EFL learner, therefore, is probably not technical language as such, but the language framework in which the technical expressions are placed. Apart from certain typical grammatical and rhetorical features which needn't concern us here, this non-technical framework will probably consist of two kinds of language: first, basic lexical items such as those listed in the General Service List (see above, p. 15), and secondly other sub-technical words and expressions typical of academic discourse (that is, words such as *ratio*, *approximate*, *hence*, etc.) which the subject specialist may assume that the student should already know.

STRUCTURE AND CONTENT

A more basic kind of distinction that is often made is between *structure* words and *content* words. Structure words may be considered as part of the grammar of the language; they are almost 'empty' of meaning when considered in isolation. If we take a word like *do* in the sentence *Do you often go for a walk at this time?* we can see that its main functions are grammatical: as a marker of the question form and as a marker of tense. Modal verbs (such as *do*, *may*, *can*, etc.), pronouns, conjunctions, prepositions, and certain adverbs (e.g. *very*, *rather*, etc.) are often put in this category. Content words are nouns, verbs, adjectives and adverbs formed from adjectives (e.g. *beautifully*). The list of content words is open-ended: new nouns and verbs are often coined to name new things or processes, and the same is true of adjectives and adverbs.

MEANING

Until now, we have been assuming that it is important to 'teach the meaning' of a word, without specifying very closely what 'teach the meaning' implies. We have just seen that some words like *do* can only, in some of their uses, be given a meaning with certainty when they are used in a context: and the more common a word is, the more likely this is to be true. In this way, we have seen above (P. 14) how the word *head* can *denote* ('mean') several things. Usually, in elementary classes, we try to teach words which have a clear, *concrete denotation*: something that can be seen or touched. So we often present nouns like *desk*, *blackboard*, *chair*, *table*, *teacher*, *student*; verbs like *sit*, *stand*, *walk*, *write*, *read*; adjectives like *big*, *small*, *round*, *square*, *red*, *green*; and so on.

As the student's command of the language improves, he will discover that even these 'straightforward' words can have a wide *range of denotations* according to the context. The word *table* for example may be discovered in contexts like these (the examples and quotation are from the *Longman Dictionary of Contemporary English*):

(1) *The waiter told us that, if we wished, we could choose something from the cold table.* (i.e. a display of cold food, such as salads etc.);

(2) *John's stories kept the whole table amused.* (i.e. everyone sitting at the table);

(3) *There is a table of contents at the front of this dictionary.* (i.e. list);

(4) *The children were learning their tables.* ('list which young children repeat to learn what number results when a number from 1 to 12 is multiplied by any of the numbers from 1 to 12')

(5) *The President is at table now but he'll see you when he's finished eating.* (i.e. *at table* = having a meal).

These are only some of the possible meanings of the noun *table*; there is also a verb *to table* with several meanings.

Most common words have a wide denotative range; technical words tend to have a narrower denotative range, i.e. they usually have one very specific meaning, and this is another thing which makes them easier to learn. Some words, of course, have a common meaning and also a technical meaning: an example is the common word *shock* (a favourite word with journalists!) which has several popular meanings, but also a technical meaning (in medicine: 'a state of bodily collapse or near collapse caused by circulatory failure or sudden lowering of the blood pressure, as from severe bleeding, burns, fright etc.', *Collins English Dictionary* [CED]).

CONNOTATION

What is the difference between being *slim* and *thin*, or even *skinny*? What is the difference between a *fat* baby and a *plump* one? Denotatively, that is, in terms of who they are referring to, there may be no difference at all: the slim person, the thin person and the skinny person may all be the same weight (or even the same person!). The choice of one phrase rather than the other will probably indicate how the speaker *feels* about the person in question.

Certain words are chosen because they convey some kind of feeling or judgement. If you approve of the way in which someone sticks to his opinions you may applaud the fact that he is *resolute* or *determined*; to someone for whom this kind of behaviour is awkward or a nuisance, the same person may be *stubborn*, *obstinate* or even *pig-headed*. We say therefore that words like *skinny*, *fat*, *stubborn*, *obstinate* and *pig-headed* tend to have unfavourable connotations; whereas words like *slim*, *resolute* or *determined* tend to be used with intended favourable connotations.

Rather similar to the connotations of a word are its *associations*, but whereas connotations relate to the system of the language, associations relate more to the individual or the culture. So, for example, while words like *father* or *home* generally have favourable associations for most people, they may have unfavourable associations for someone who had a very unhappy homelife. A word like *market* may have very different associations for someone coming from (perhaps) a rural area in a tropical country, as opposed to a city dweller in Britain. Similarly it may be very difficult to convey the associations that *countryside* had for a nature poet like Wordsworth to a child to whom wild, uncultivated areas are more dangerous and threatening than otherwise.

Clearly there is not much to be done about the private associations which words have for individuals, but the teacher may well feel that associations which relate the culture of the target language, and certainly the connotations of a particular word are part of the 'meaning' which has to be learned.

RELATIONSHIPS BETWEEN WORDS

The meanings of certain words are so closely related that they are often confused by the learner. This is especially true of words with *reciprocal meanings* such as words like *borrow/lend*, *bring/take* (also *fetch*), or *imply/infer*. In the case of *imply* (*the speaker implied* [that someting was so]) and *infer* (*from what the speaker said, I inferred* [that something was so]), the distinction is so fine, even for educated native speakers, that many dictionaries now list *imply* as one of the meanings of *infer*! (In doing this, of course, the dictionary writers are not doing anything wrong: they are simply doing their job of recording actual usage, however much such usage may offend those who feel that the *imply/infer* distinction is a useful one which ought to be preserved.)

Another teaching problem arises with words which are in the same rough area of meaning or *semantic field*. One example is the words which can be used instead of the noun *horse*, such as *colt* ('male horse or pony under the age of 4', CED), *filly* ('female horse or pony under the age of 4'), *foal* ('young of a horse or related animal') *mare* ('adult female horse'), *pony* ('any of various breeds of small horse, usually under 14.2 hands'), *palamino* ('golden horse with a cream or white mane and tail'), *roan* ('horse or light brown to brownish orange colour'), etc. It will be seen that these words are used to distinguish (or *mark*) different kinds of horse according to sex, age, height, colour and so on. Just how complex such relationships can be is illustrated in Figure 1.1 (from Lehrer, 1974), which shows some of the distinctions made in English under the general heading *cooking*. The problem is not, of course, that such distinctions exist, but that they may not exist in the mother tongue of the learner, or, if they exist, the distinctions may be made in a different way.

Thus an English speaker learning Spanish must learn to use different verbs for 'I *am* a student' (*ser*) and 'I *am* tired' (*estar*), while in French there is a distinction between 'I *know* how to speak English' (*savoir*) and 'I *know* Mr Smith' (*connaître*). In the reverse direction, a German student learning English has to learn to distinguish between *chair* (furniture for sitting on with a back) and *stool* (the same, without a back), for both of which only one word is necessary in German (*Stuhl*) (see Leech, 1974, p. 30). The business of distinguishing between words in the same semantic field is at the same time a fascinating and exasperating topic for intermediate and advanced learners.

	Water	Oil or fat	Vapour	Amount of liquid	Kind of source of heat	Cooking action	Special utensil	Special additional purpose	Cooking appeal
boil₁	+	–	–						
boil₂ (full)	+	–	–			[Vigorous]			
simmer	+	–	–			(Gentle)		[To soften]	[Slow]
stew	+	–	–			(Gentle)		[To preserve shape]	[Fast]
poach	+	+	–			[Gentle]			
braise	+	–	–	[Small]			(Pot with lid)		
steam	+	+	+				(Rack, sieve)		
fry	–	+	*				(Frying pan)		
sauté	–	+	*	[Small]					
French fry deep fry	–	–	*	[Large]					
broil	–	–	*	*	[Radiant]	*			
grill	–	–	*	*	[Radiant]	*	(Grill, griddle)		
barbecue charcoal	–	–	*	*	[Radiant (Hot coals)]	*			
bake	–	–	*	*	[Conducted]	*	(Oven)		
roast	–	–	*	*	[Radiant or Conducted]	*			

+   means that this component is involved.
–   means that this component is not involved.
*   means that this component does not apply.

Fig. 1.1   Distinctions made in English among words relating to cooking methods (Lehrer, 1974)

PRODUCTIVE AND RECEPTIVE VOCABULARY

An important distinction which is often made is between *productive* and *receptive* vocabulary. Everyone who learns a foreign language is usually able to recognize many more words than he can produce. It is much more difficult to produce a word correctly: one has to pronounce or spell it in the right way, use it in the correct grammatical form, use it appropriately with the correct words coming before and after it, and so on. It may therefore be important for a teacher to decide which words he wishes a student to *produce* correctly, and which words he wishes him merely to *recognize*.

Special problems of productive vocabulary

Producing (speaking or writing) words in the target language makes much greater demands in many ways of the learner. Of course, in producing vocabulary the learner has one advantage in that he is usually in a position to choose which words he wishes to use: whereas in receptive vocabulary (as in reading or listening) he has to handle whatever language the native speaker may 'throw at' him. There is a lot more work involved in giving a student a productive vocabulary of 2000 words, which the student is able to use correctly in a wide range of contexts, as opposed to, say, a reading vocabulary of 2000 words.

Nevertheless, having chosen to use a particular word, he risks being misunderstood unless he uses it not only with the correct 'meaning' (as we have just discussed) but also:

(1)   with the correct pronunciation, spelling, and stress;
(2)   with the correct form;
(3)   in the appropriate collocation.

PRONUNCIATION AND SPELLING

These aspects of a word are related in English, because it is the comparative unpredictability of the English sound–symbol relationship which causes so many problems. Learners are puzzled by words which have very different forms but are pronounced identically, e.g. *genes/jeans*, *break/brake*, etc; and also by words which are very similar in form but pronounced differently, e.g. *bough*, *tough*, *though*, etc.

Since the rules of English pronunciation are so complex, occasionally this leads the student to having a wild lunge at a pronunciation which is grotesquely wrong. More important, however, are the systematic sound confusions such as /i/ and /i:/ which cause *bit/beat*, *dip/deep* etc. to be pronounced in the same way (usually with /i:/). In some contexts this kind of confusion can lead to a complete breakdown in communication, as when on a trip abroad I heard the question 'Do you like snacks?' as 'Do you like snakes?'. The resulting conversation is perhaps best left to the reader's imagination.

Spelling mistakes less frequently cause lack of understanding, and are more often simply a give-away of the writer's status as a learner. Again it is the lack of fit between the sound and the spelling system which causes problems: the *-or/-ar/-er* and *-able/ible* groups of suffixes, for example, are pronounced in exactly the same way. It may comfort learners to know that native speakers sometimes tend to be as confused as they are so that, for example, *adviser* and *advisor* are both acceptable spellings of the same word. (Unfortunately for the learner this free-and-easy attitude is extended to only a very few words!)

STRESS

As far as intelligibility is concerned, getting the correct stress is often extremely important, since, in English, the stress pattern of a word determines its pronunciation of the individual vowel sounds: only in the stressed syllable does the vowel tend to get its full value, the other unstressed vowels tending to be neutralized. Thus if words like *re'ceptive* and *'recognize* are stressed on the wrong syllables, they can become almost impossible for the native speaker to catch in a flow of speech, especially when (as often happens) other words in the learner's speech are also being wrongly stressed. Word stress patterns are often used systematically in various ways, e.g. to distinguish between nouns and verbs as in *'record* (noun) and *re'cord* (verb).

CORRECT FORM

It is, of course, possible to 'know' a word, without necessarily knowing how to use it in all its various forms. So, for example, a learner will know to use the adjective *big* for some time before he learns its comparative and superlative forms *bigger* and *biggest*. With a verb like *sing*, the form *sings* will be learnt early on; *sang* might be learnt later, and the participle form *sung* later still. With nouns, however, we would expect the singular and plural forms to be available almost at the same time.

These areas might seem more properly dealt with in the sphere of grammar rather than vocabulary. The use of suffixes and prefixes and formation of compound nouns are, however, clearly in the area of vocabulary development. In working out the meaning of new words, it is useful for the learner to be trained to see the common element in *friendship*, *membership* and *dictatorship*, where the common suffix *-ship* conveys the idea of 'state of being or having a ...'; between *useful* and *useless*, where the suffixes *-ful* and *-less* denote opposite qualities, and so on. But whereas *useful* has as its opposite *useless*, the opposite of *successful* is not *successless* but *unsuccessful*, and *delightful* has no derived opposite at all: one would have to find a different word (perhaps *horrible* might do).

Similarly with compound nouns, the surface similarities conceal many differences in the 'deep structure' of such words, so that *headmaster* = the master *who is* head (of a school), *arrowhead* = the head *of* an arrow, *armchair* = a chair *with arms*, *bookstall* — a stall (stand) *where* books, etc. *are sold*, and so on.

COGNATES AND 'FALSE FRIENDS'

We mentioned earlier how learners who speak a language that is related to English may have an advantage because many words in both languages have the same derivation and are therefore similar in form ('cognates'). Thus the Spanish *método* is clearly related to the English *method*, the Portuguese *equipamento* to the English word *equipment* and so on. Moreover English and the learner's mother tongue are often related in a systematic way. For example,

English words ending in -*action* may often be 'translated' directly into Spanish words ending in -*ación*, so that *organization* is *organisación*, *nation* is *nación*, etc.   Speaking a language which has this kind of close relationship in certain areas with English is certainly an advantage, but it is not an unmixed blessing. Words often have very similar forms in related languages, but totally different meanings: these are the words known to the language learners as 'false friends'. Examples like these will be familiar to speakers of European languages: *actually* does not mean 'happening just now' (as in French *actuellement*), but 'really, truly'; *cave* means 'a kind of cavern' not 'a basement' (French *cave*); *confused* means 'perplexed' more often than 'embarrassed' (French *confus*); *to edit* does not mean 'to publish' (French *éditer*); and so on. Some words partially overlap: for example, the English and French meanings of *amateur* (spelt the same in both languages) are partially identical in the sense of someone who is not a *professional* (in sport, etc.), but the French word also has the meaning of someone who is keen on something, e.g. 'un amateur du cinéma' (cinema lover), etc. In English, strangely enough, the Spanish loan-word *aficionado* is often used in this sense.

Although we started the chapter by noting that comparatively little has been written by language teachers on teaching vocabulary, much has been written by linguists on lexis and meaning ('semantics'). For readers who would like to read more about these subjects, some suggestions are listed below (see Further Reading).

2 The Principles of Teaching and Learning Vocabulary

We have seen in the last chapter how learning vocabulary is a rather more complex process than it might at first sight appear. To 'know' a word in a target language as well as the native speaker knows it may mean the ability to:

(a)   recognize it in its spoken or written form;
(b)   recall it at will;
(c)   relate it to an appropriate object or concept;
(d)   use it in the appropriate grammatical form;
(e)   in speech, pronounce it in a recognizable way;
(f)   in writing, spell it correctly;
(g)   use it with the words it correctly goes with, i.e. in the correct collocation;
(h)   use it at the appropriate level of formality;
(i)   be aware of its connotations and associations.

The teacher has the job of so managing the learning that the learner can do some or all of these things with the target vocabulary that is to be learnt. What are the principles on which such learning is to be based?

AIMS

First, the teacher has to be clear about his or her *aims*: how many of the things listed does the teacher expect the learner to be able to do? With which words? Unless the teacher is clear on this point, it will be difficult to assess how successful or otherwise the vocabulary learning has been.

Certain no. per lesson etc.
they ask - Trans- L. one each -
per group?

QUANTITY

Secondly, having decided on what is involved in vocabulary learning, the teacher may have to decide on the *quantity of vocabulary* to be learnt. How many new words in a lesson can the learner learn? If we mean by 'learn' that the words become part of the student's active vocabulary, then one estimate puts the number as low as around five to seven new words. Clearly the actual number will depend on a number of factors varying from class to class and learner to learner. If there are too many new words, the learner may become confused, discouraged and frustrated. For example, the 'frustration level' above which someone reading a passage in the target language will tend to give up, unless he has recourse to a dictionary, has been estimated at 10 per cent or more unknown words. However, it must be said that any figure given without reference to a specific class or individual case will not be very reliable.

The opposite case is where the learner is not 'stretched' and so makes less progress than he or she could: some people feel that the emphasis on very strict control of vocabulary in structurally graded courses has led to this fault. If he feels that his students (or some of them) could cope with a larger vocabulary input, the teacher may decide to supplement the students' vocabulary from sources other than the course-book.

NEED

Control of the amount of vocabulary inevitably means choice as to the specific items to be taught. We have already discussed some of the criteria that can be used, such as frequency, availability and learnability. In most cases the choice will be made for the teacher by the course-book or syllabus he is using. In any case, one would hope that the choice of vocabulary will relate to the aims of the course and the objectives of individual lessons. It is also possible for the teacher, in a sense, to put the responsibility of choosing the vocabulary to be taught on to the students. In other words, the student is put in a situation where he has to communicate and gets the words he needs, as he needs them, using the teacher as an informant. This reflects the informal language situation we find ourselves in when operating in a foreign language in the country where it is spoken. If we are fortunate enough to have a native speaker of the language nearby, we ask him or her 'How do you say ...' or 'What is the name for this?' The vocabulary is then presented in response to our own needs and interests, and we are perhaps more likely to remember it. It might, therefore, be a good thing to try to bring about this situation in our language classrooms. The student should feel that he *needs* the target word, just as he would in a situation outside the classroom.

FREQUENT EXPOSURE AND REPETITION

It is seldom, however, that we remember a new word simply by hearing it once. There has to be a certain amount of repetition until there is evidence that the student has learned the target word. The simplest way of checking that this learning has been done is by seeing whether the student can recognize the target word and identify its meaning. If the word has to be part of the learner's productive vocabulary, he must be given the opportunity to use it, as often as is necessary for him to recall it at will, with the correct stress and pronunciation. It is not enough, however, that this should happen only in one lesson: since the learner is exposed to a large number of words, the words he is meant to remember should crop up at regular intervals in later lessons.

MEANINGFUL PRESENTATION

As well as the *form* of the word, the learner must have a clear and specific understanding of what it denotes or refers to, i.e. its meaning – although, as we have seen in the previous chapter, 'meaning' involves many other things as well. This requires that the word is presented in such a way that its denotation or reference is perfectly clear and unambiguous, which is not always an easy task.

SITUATION PRESENTATION

In the previous chapter we saw that the choice of words can vary according to the situation in which we are speaking (e.g. whether on board ship or on dry land), and according to how well we know the person to whom we are speaking (from informal to very formal). It seems sensible that a student should learn words in the situation in which they are appropriate.

PRESENTATION IN CONTEXT

Words very seldom occur in isolation. We have seen how important it is for the learner to know the usual collocations that the word occurs in. So from the very beginning the word must appear in its natural environment as it were, among the words it normally collocates with.

LEARNING VOCABULARY IN THE MOTHER TONGUE AND IN THE TARGET LANGUAGE

At this point perhaps we should pause and see how the principles which we have established so far relate to the learning of vocabulary in the L1 (or mother tongue) and L2 (target language). Nearly everyone in his lifetime acquires a fairly large vocabulary in his mother tongue; very large, compared to what most foreign language learners would aspire to. How is this large vocabulary achieved? First, there is felt need: in the L1 'knowing the words' is a matter of survival, or at least of social competence – this basic kind of need does not exist in most foreign language-learning programmes, and so a paler, less realistic version of it usually has to be engineered in some way.

Secondly, the L1 learner mostly controls his own rate of learning. In a protective environment, adults are tolerant of children's ignorance of language: the *child* is more likely to feel anger and frustration in this respect. So he learns what he needs as he needs it.

Thirdly, the L1 is exposed to an enormous quantity of his own language and has tremendous scope for repetition of what he learns.

Fourthly, the language is nearly always encountered in an appropriate situation and in the appropriate context. So he will probably not have too many problems with appropriateness or with collocation.

Fifthly, since words are learnt as they arise out of a felt need in a particular situation, they usually have a clear denotation. Young children do have problems with denotation, however: thus, at an early stage, a child may equate the word *dog* with any four-legged animal – only later will he narrow it down, and discover other names for other types of animal.

Of course there is no necessary reason why the vocabulary of the L2 should be learnt in the same way as the L1 vocabulary: after all, the circumstances are very different, and, since the time available for learning the L2 is almost invariably very much shorter, then short cuts will have to be taken. It is interesting to note, however, that many of the principles which we have derived from our discussion of the linguistic background in Chapter 1 apply equally well to the mother tongue.

INFERENCING ('GUESSING') PROCEDURES IN VOCABULARY LEARNING

There is one aspect of both L1 and L2 learning which demands comment. With mature L1 speakers and competent speakers of a foreign language, the observer is struck by the difference between the number of words which the speaker could have been *taught*, and the number of words which he *knows*. Estimates of the vocabulary of educated native speakers vary very widely: many estimates of recognition (i.e. passive) vocabulary come out at between 100,000 and 200,000 words, including words derived from the same root (like *glad* and *gladly*). Even very conservative estimates put the number at 40,000 words. How many of those had he/she been specifically taught the meaning of? A small percentage, one would guess. Very many language-teaching programmes aspire to only about 2000 words. Are the remaining words learnt from a dictionary? Almost certainly not. If the meanings have not been supplied by outside sources, as it were, then where have they been found?

The answer is, of course, that we guess the meanings of words by hearing them used in a certain situation, or sometimes by reading them in a certain context and guessing their meaning from the context. Usually it is clear in a situation what particular thing someone is referring to; in a written context a bit more detective work may be called for.

As an example, we may take *A Clockwork Orange*, the famous novel by Anthony Burgess. This novel is set in some time in the future and the author imagines that the English language has changed, like everything else. He therefore freely uses words which are not part of the present English language: in the first few paragraphs the number of these 'new' words runs to almost 10 per cent of the total number of words (i.e. dangerously close to 'frustration' level, according to some). Since this is a very widely read book one must presume that the vast majority of the readers can cope with, or at least tolerate, this large number of words, the meanings of which they have to guess (there being no dictionary of Burgess's new English available!).

In many cases it is not really too difficult. Let us take the 'new' word *goloss*, for example (page references are to the Penguin edition, 1972):

(p. 7) 'The stereo was on and you got the idea that the singer's *goloss* was moving from one part of the bar to another, flying up to the ceiling then swooping down again and whizzing from wall to wall';
(p. 8) 'but he said: "Yes? What is it?" in a very loud teacher-type *goloss*, as if he was trying to show us he wasn't *poogly*' (= afraid);
(p. 19) 'so I said in a very refined manner of speech, a real gentleman's *goloss*: "Pardon, madam, most sorry to disturb you …"'.

It is easy to deduce that *goloss* must mean 'voice'. It may be interesting for the reader to work out precisely what clues he or she used to infer the meaning. Obviously the general sense of the contexts help; some readers may also have made a connection with the form of the word *goloss* and other words such as *glossary* (= list of definitions), which show that the meaning has probably some connection with language or speech.

These clues, that is, both from the general sense of the context and also the form or structure of the word itself, are probably the kind of clues that most readers use to guess the meanings of unknown words without recourse to a dictionary.

Another aspect of L1 vocabulary learning is that the mother-tongue speaker learns to be content with *approximate meaning*: in other words, he is satisfied with a meaning which makes sense of the context. Thus someone reading a historical novel set in the nineteenth century and coming across a reference to 'the aristocrats riding along the country roads in their magnificent broughams, barouches and clarences' will probably guess that these are all names of horse-drawn carriages of some kind, and be content with that: only if he is curious will he check up a dictionary to discover the exact differences between them – the brougham was a closed carriage; the clarence also closed but with a glass front; the barouche had a retractable hood over the rear half of the passenger's compartment. It is unlikely that knowing the precise differences between these old-fashioned carriages would add anything to the reader's understanding or enjoyment of the story. Similarly, one has seen overseas editions of R. L. Stevenson's adventure story *Treasure Island* containing diagrams of sailing ships with every part meticulously labelled. Is it necessary to know more about the *mizzenmast* than that it is one of the masts on a sailing ship, or the *topgallant sail* that it is a kind of sail? Most young readers who are reading the story properly, that is with enjoyment, will be too caught up in the story to bother about such details. In the secret service there is a principle called the 'need-to-know' principle – in other words agents are not told more than they need to know in case they get caught and betray their comrades. Perhaps in vocabulary learning the 'need-to-know' principle could also be applied: students should not be told more about the meanings of words than they need to know to understand the context.

In a way, what we have been saying about how vocabulary is acquired should be encouraging, since it shows us that learners can be their own best teachers, if they are exposed to the target language in an appropriate way. It is unfortunate that most learners of a foreign language are not exposed to it in situations outside the classroom as native speakers are. They can, however, be exposed to the target language in the form of *appropriate* reading matter. The word *appropriate* has been stressed, because we have already made the point that if the material is too difficult, with too many new words, then the reader becomes 'frustrated' and gives up.

Anyone who has been in charge of a library where intermediate-level learners have the run of the shelves, will have come across the sad case of the overambitious student who takes down an unsimplified classic – often by Dickens. When the student returns the book, the first page will have perhaps twenty new words underlined (another bad habit!); the second page, fifteen words; the third, ten. Is the student's command of English vocabulary improving dramatically – or is he just getting tired and disheartened? Alas, the latter answer is more probably the right one!

Students should be given access to books *which are within their vocabulary range*. This probably means that a *class* library is preferable to a *school* library, as far as English readers are concerned. Also, in any class, there is probably a fairly wide range in the vocabulary levels of different students – so each class library should have a range of readers: some easy enough for the weakest student, others advanced enough for the better students. This means that, as a working rule, the number of readers available should be at least the number of students in the class, plus 50 per cent.

Fortunately for the modern EFL teacher there is available on the market, a wide range of cheap, attractively produced and carefully graded readers. At one time the only kind of graded readers available were simplified versions of the classics: the first such book I had to use was *Lorna Doone* simplified down to a vocabulary of 500 words! Many of the titles now available have been written specially for learners; others are slightly simplified versions of thrillers and adventure stories, where the quality of the language is often less important than the interest of the plot.

If at all possible, the EFL teachers should make a selection of such books available to their students. They can be allowed to start reading them silently in class, and encouraged to continue reading them at home. If the reading programme catches on, the teacher can keep a record of how many books each student is reading, and which titles. This can be simply done by the student filling up a card for each book read, with the author, title, and a few comments. Only brief comments should be required: one does not want to punish the keen reader by forcing him to write an essay for his pains!

Graded magazines, appropriate to different stages of learner, are also available, almost always presented in a lively and entertaining format: another invaluable way of painlessly expanding vocabulary. (For more information about graded readers and graded magazines, see Further Reading.)

3   *Vocabulary in the Classroom*

Let us start by looking at the first few minutes of the very first lesson which a group of learners are being given. The class is an adult class where all the learners have the same mother tongue. When the teacher is speaking in the mother tongue, her words will be printed *in italics*. Words written in ordinary (Roman) type are said in the target language (English).

Teacher: Good morning. Welcome to your first lesson in English. I know that most of you have come to this class because you want to be able to speak in English when you go to visit Britain. So most of our activity will be talking and not writing, especially at the beginning. I don't want you to write. Let's begin. (T draws a matchstick figure of a girl on the blackboard.) This is Mary. (T writes the name 'Mary' on the blackboard.) Mary. This is Mary. (T then draws the matchstick figure of a boy.) This is John. (T writes the name 'John' on the blackboard.) John. This is John. (T points to the girl.) This is Mary. (T points to the boy.) This is John. They are walking. (T uses her fingers in a 'walking' movement.) They are walking. They meet. (T uses fingers of both hands in walking movement from opposite sides of the blackboard until they meet in the middle.) John says 'Hello'. (Pause) 'Hello'. (Pause) 'Hello'. *Now repeat after me.* Hello.
   Class: Hello.
   T: Hello.
   C: Hello.
   T: John says, 'Hello, Mary'. (Pause) 'Hello Mary'.
   C: Hello, Mary.
   T: Mary says, 'Hello, John'.

C: Hello, John.
T: Hello, John.
C: Hello, John.
(T indicates one half of the class, Group 1.)
T: You are John.
(T indicates other half of the class, Group 2.)
T: You are Mary.
T: (pointing to Group 1): Hello, Mary.
Gp 1: Hello, Mary.
T: (pointing to Group 2): Hello, John.
Gp 2: Hello, John.
T then points to some individual members of each group, getting them to repeat either 'Hello, John' or 'Hello, Mary' as appropriate.

Before you read on any further, perhaps it would be a good idea for you first to make up your own mind about some things before we discuss them.

(1) What do you think the teacher's objectives are for this part of the lesson – in other words, what is she trying to teach?
(2) What principles for teaching vocabulary that we have discussed so far are illustrated in this little bit of teaching?
(3) Can you distinguish in this extract between *productive* and *receptive* vocabulary?
(4) Some of the things said by the teacher are in the mother tongue. What is the mother tongue used *for* in this case? What are your views on this?

Since the teacher was teaching a group of adults who are mostly learning English so that they can speak to native English speakers when they visit Britain, she had to teach them common greetings, and this is what she was doing in this extract. She was teaching situationally, but she did not tell the students what they were going to learn, and neither did she use translation. The students had to guess the meaning.

Of course, the teacher gave them some help. The help given took the form of:

(1)   the drawings on the blackboard: these established that two people were involved, a boy and a girl;
(2)   the use of mime, by using her fingers to indicate a walking movement and the act of meeting;
(3)   writing the names on the blackboard, which helped to identify the boy and girl.

The teacher also made use of what we might broadly call *background knowledge*, in this case taking the particular form of *cultural expectation*. When two people meet we would naturally expect them to greet one another, so it seems reasonable for the class to assume that that is what is happening in this particular case.

The teacher obviously wishes to ensure that the students not only understand the language used, but can also produce it themselves. So she has built in opportunities for language production. What methods has she used for this? Were there any others that she could have used? Perhaps you might like to take a few moments to think about this.

The methods used by the teacher here were basically classroom repetition, group to group repetition, and individual repetition. Some other methods that could have been used were pair work (students working in pairs), chain drill (the student at the extreme right of the class turns round and greets the student on his left, who answers the greeting, then greets the student on *his* left, and so on), and pair work in front of the class (where students come out in twos to exchange greetings). Possibly the teacher would have got round to using some of these techniques, after the students had learned some more exchanges which would naturally follow on from 'Hello', such as 'How are you?' – 'Fine, thanks', 'And how are you?' – 'Oh, not too bad', etc.

There are other questions one might ask oneself about this bit of teaching. The first one is: how *accurate* a grasp of the meaning of this particular greeting did the students have? After all, a range of greetings exist in English, as in other languages: *Good morning*; *Good evening*; *hi*, etc., all appropriate to different situations and different levels of formality. Most teachers would, in fact, be happy if the students have grasped the *approximate meaning* of *Hello*: an informal greeting used between people who are on first-name terms with each other. The distinctions between words with related meanings appropriate in different situations can come later.

A second question might be: how could the teacher be *sure* that all the students had grasped the meaning of the language presented, and that some of them were not just repeating without understanding? The answer here is probably that she couldn't be absolutely certain: but most experienced teachers can sense from the students' response whether they are bewildered or not.

One obvious method of checking understanding might be simply to ask the students to 'translate' either into the mother tongue or into simpler English: 'What do you think X means?'. However, in the case of an expression which is going to be frequently encountered in class (such as 'Hello'), the teacher may prefer to take a chance that even the dullest students will very quickly sense the meaning.

In teaching the meaning of words, therefore, especially at the elementary stage, teachers try to establish a direct link between the word and the meaning, either by using 'realia' (i.e. real things such as tables, desks, etc.), drawings, photographs or (as in the lesson we have just been discussing) blackboard drawings or mime.

Let us now move from the very elementary level of teaching that we have been discussing to a much more advanced level (college/ university level, in fact), where we shall have a look at the teaching of vocabulary in a *written context*. The passage that we are going to look at is used in one of the SRA Language Laboratory speed reading cards, level III B. Here is the passage:

The works of Galileo Galilei (1564–1642) capture the true and living spirit of scientific inquiry. Galileo lived in a Europe hidebound by the centuries-old cultural philosophy of Aristotle and the astronomy of Ptolemy, in which man and the earth were thought to be the pinnacle of creation and the centre of the universe. One who deviated from this orthodoxy, enforced by church and state, did so at his peril. Galileo dared. He courageously taught science as he observed it, refuting Aristotle;

and his 'Astronomical Message' of 1610 reported what he saw through a homemade telescope – with calculations and conclusions damaging to Ptolemaic astronomy. And, at the age of seventy, Galileo was threatened with torture unless he repudiated his scientific opinions.

Before looking at the lesson transcript, we might pause here to establish a few points. Of course it is difficult to answer any questions about how something should be taught when you do not know the class involved, and anyway you might feel that this is a passage that you would never wish to use as teaching material. Nevertheless, I think that the questions that follow are answerable in general terms.

(1)　At what stage in discussing this passage with the class would you start teaching individual vocabulary items?

(2)　How would you choose which items to teach? (You do not have to specify the exact words you would choose. Simply think of *how* you choose which items to teach.)

(3)　What are the main methods that you would use to teach them?

The answers to these questions are obviously interrelated: so, for example, the point at which you decide to teach a vocabulary item may depend on how you have decided to teach it. First of all, you must decide which items are likely to cause problems with the class. At the elementary and lower-intermediate stages this may not be too difficult. For one thing, if you are using a course-book, there may be a list of new words in each chapter located in the teacher's book, or even in the student's book. At the more advanced stages, it is more difficult to predict which words the students do not know, and the teacher often has to rely on his own judgement.

Of course it is always possible to get this information from the students. Students can be asked to read through the passage and note down the words they don't know. The unknown words can either be dealt with in class by the teacher, or the students can check them up in their dictionaries. This approach has one big advantage – it relates the vocabulary teaching to what the students need to know. But many teachers would argue that it also has several disadvantages. You might like to think about what they could be, and we shall come back to this question after we have discussed some other issues.

Let us assume, for the time being, that the teacher has identified some words that the students may not know. What is he going to do with them? This will depend on the teacher's objectives for the lesson. If we are thinking about a comprehension lesson, we might say that usually the teacher's main objective in such a lesson is to make sure that the students have at least a *general understanding* of the passage. This comes first, and the understanding of individual words is therefore of secondary importance.

This makes sense for at least two reasons:

(1)   It is an important aim in any EFL reading programme to train students to go for the overall meaning of the article or book that they are reading, and not allow themselves to be put off or distracted by individual words that they don't know.

(2)   The meaning of an individual word depends on the general meaning of the passage: we have already seen how most common words have a vast range of denotations; which denotation is the appropriate one will depend on the meaning of the passage as a whole.

These two points are clearly related, and it is worth while dwelling on them a little bit more. There is a tendency among language learners to look at the meaning of a passage as if it were built up of individual units (words) each one of which has to be decoded before they can proceed on to the next one. In fact what happens in normal reading is something very different: the reader samples the text, continually making guesses about what the meaning might be. These guesses are either confirmed as the reader reads on, or not; if they are not, then the reader has to go back ('regress') and read part of the text again. (For further information about the reading process, see Frank Smith, *Understanding Reading*: Holt, Rinehart, 1971).

We see then that word-decoding is something we want to discourage. In dealing with a comprehension passage, therefore, the usual procedure is to ask questions which establish the general sense of the passage first, and then to come on to questions about the meanings of individual words.

In dealing with individual words, the teacher really has a choice of four techniques:

(1)   To explain the meaning of the difficult words, either by translation, or by giving an explanation or 'gloss' in simpler English. This is the procedure adopted in many course books where there is a vocabulary list or glossary with the passage.

(2)   To simply ignore the word, unless a question about it is raised by the students. This does not necessarily mean that the teacher is not 'doing his duty'. As we have seen, it is not always necessary to understand the meaning of every single word in a passage to get the general sense of the passage.

(3)   To get the students to check up the target words in their dictionaries.

(4)   To try to get the meaning of the word from the class, and if they don't know it already, to try to get them to guess or *infer* the meaning.

Although it takes most class time, the last technique may well be the most efficient in the long run. We have already said (in Chapter 2) that native speakers, or competent speakers of a foreign language, have mostly expanded their vocabulary by reading words in context and making intelligent guesses at their meaning. In most language teaching programmes, the teacher can hope to teach the student only a fraction of the words that he or she is going to need to know. It seems, therefore, to be a good use of class time to spend some time on showing students how meaning can be inferred from context. So in teaching a reading passage, the primary aim might be to get at the general sense of the passage, but a secondary aim might well be to show how the meanings of certain unknown words can be inferred or guessed at.

Eliciting the meanings of unknown words is a time-consuming process, and also not all words can be guessed from context; so the teacher will have to choose carefully those words which he thinks he can lead the students to an understanding of, and he will also have to decide how he is going to lead the students to that kind of understanding.

If there are any words which are essential to the understanding of the passage, but whose meaning cannot be easily inferred, then the teacher may well decide simply to explain them to the students either by providing a gloss (explanation) beforehand, or by explaining them as they arise. If the gloss is written or printed, then it should be displayed where the reader can easily see it and not, say, at the back of the book.

We have already mentioned the possibility of students checking up words in their dictionaries, and certainly the proper and efficient use of a dictionary is something that students ought to be trained in, if only because the dictionary helps the student to be independent of the teacher and the classroom. Nevertheless, it could be argued that recourse to the dictionary should *not* be typical of every reading period. For one thing it may encourage the tendency to concentrate on individual words rather than overall meaning. Also, the learner may not explore those possibilities of using the context to decode meaning that we are trying to encourage. Over-frequent use of the dictionary slows up the flow of reading, and makes the passage more boring to read and perhaps even less easy to understand because concentration is interrupted. Obviously one would never ban the dictionary from the classroom, but there may be lessons when the teacher may want it to be closed, while other pathways to meaning are followed.

We earlier mentioned the possibility of simply asking the learners which words they don't know and explaining them. It should be clear now why this is not always a sensible move, more especially at the beginning of the lesson. We could list the following problems:

(1) Leaving the choice of vocabulary to be explained makes the planning of the lesson more difficult: the teacher does not know what is going to come up.

(2)   More seriously, it undermines the reading strategy by overemphasizing the meanings of *words* at the expense of the overall meaning of the passage.
(3)   It makes it difficult for the teacher to establish his priorities of: words to be explained, words to be elicited and words that can be ignored.
(4)   It makes it more difficult for the teacher to use the general sense of the passage to elicit the meaning of individual words.

So we can see that it is probably better to leave this to the end of the lesson, after the teacher has achieved the objectives that he has set himself. Finding out what still puzzles the learners (or some of them) at that stage can be very valuable feedback to the teacher, as well as useful for satisfying the learner's legitimate curiosity. Even then, of course, the learners should, as far as possible, be encouraged to work out the meaning for themselves.

Let us now return to the passage on Galileo, which you may wish to glance at again (see p. 39). In this case the words which the teacher thought that he could elicit were *inquiry*, *hidebound*, *pinnacle*, *courageously* and *refuting*. What do you think of his choice? What are the problems involved in eliciting these words?

We are now going to look at what happened when the teacher tried to elicit the first of these words, *inquiry*. At different points in the extract you will see numbers in sequence, starting with (1). When you come to each of the numbers, you might find it useful to stop and ask yourself what the teacher seems to be getting at, that is, why is he asking this particular question or making this particular statement. (Note that this is a micro-lesson concerned only with elicitation of word-meaning, so the teacher is not concerned at this point with teaching the comprehension of the general meaning of the passage: *T* = tutor; *S1–S5* = individual students; *Ss* = several students.)

T: In the first sentence it says that 'The words of Galileo Galilei (1564–1642) capture the true and living spirit of scientific inquiry.' Well, we are interested in this word *inquiry* (1). Can I ask you first of all, who was Galileo? (2).

S4: He was a scientist.

T: What is it that scientists do? What is their job?

S2: They makc discoveries and ...

S1: They invent.

T: Yes, I think that is the end of the point of what they are after (3). They want to make discoveries.

S5: They do research.

T: They do research as well don't they? Right. So in order to make their discoveries, they have to do research. Right. Any other way of doing research? What are they doing when they are doing research? (4).

S5: Doing experiments.

T: Doing experiments. That's right. O.K.

Now, it says that Galileo 'captured the true and living spirit of scientific inquiry'. Since we know what scientists' jobs are, what do you think that inquiry might mean? (5).

S4: Interest.

T: Interest. 'He captured the true and living spirit of 'scientific interest' (6). That's not what we said the scientists' job was? (7).

S4: To do research.

T: Right, O.K. So what if he captures the true and living spirit of scientific inquiry? What is that? What do we mean?

Ss: They make discoveries.

T: Yes, I'm thinking of the process that leads up to discovery.

S1: Invention.

T: Yes, well, invention and discovery are both the end of what he does. What must he do before he discovers?

S5: Investigation.

T: He must investigate. So we guess that inquiry means something like 'investigation' (8). O.K., let's go on.

The reader should note that this is not intended as a *model* of how inference of word-meaning should be handled; there are various possible criticisms of this piece of teaching that you might like to discuss, one being the length of time that it took the teacher to get an answer that he felt he could accept. It is, however, interesting in that it reveals several techniques that are often used by teachers in eliciting word-meaning.

The first technique is at (1). What the teacher seems to be doing here is *focusing* the students' attention, first of all on the part of the passage that is going to be discussed, and then, more narrowly, on the specific word whose meaning is to be inferred. The students now know that the objective of the teaching has to do with this word *inquiry*.

This is perhaps just as well, since the teacher rather abruptly switches to asking a question about Galileo. In asking this question, the teacher might be appealing to the students' *understanding of the context* or, perhaps more likely in this case, their *background knowledge*. His strategy is obvious: unless the students know what sort of person Galileo was, they are not likely to be able to guess the meanings of the words to be taught.

The teacher is fortunate in that his students know that Galileo was a scientist, and obviously have a good idea of what scientists do. The first few responses, however, concentrate on the *results* of their inquiry (that is, discovery or invention) rather than the *process*. However, note that, as under (3), the teacher is receptive to his students' suggestions, even though they are not quite what he wants.

When he gets the answer that 'They do research', he must feel that he is close, and asks more questions in this area (4). When he gets the reply 'doing experiments', he feels that he is close enough to focus the students' attention on the target item once more, and ask them to make a guess at the meaning (5). Unfortunately for him, he does not get an acceptable answer ('interest'). Again, he does not criticize the answer, but puts it in context (6), and shows that it is not acceptable (7). By retracing his steps, he leads the students through the 'invention' and 'discovery' answers again, until at last he gets an answer that he finds acceptable: 'investigation' (8).

One thing worth noting about this piece of teaching is that the teacher does not give up easily. Perhaps he has carried it to an extreme, and there is not always so much time in a foreign language classroom. On the other hand, perhaps many teachers give up too easily: a few students are asked what the word might mean and if they don't know the teacher gives it to them. Probably more time ought to be spent on getting students to make 'educated guesses' at word meanings.

The two examples of classroom interaction that we have been examining are at opposite ends of the learning situation: the first one very elementary, and the second one rather advanced. Nevertheless they have certain elements in common:

(1)   In both, the learner had to be mentally alert since he had to guess at the meanings of the words being used.
(2)   In both, the learner was given enough 'input' (or information) on which to base a guess. In the first lesson the input mostly took the form of blackboard work and mime; in the second, it consisted of the other words in the passage (i.e. the general meaning of the passage), and also the learner's own background knowledge.

The main difference between the two lies in their aims: in the first the teacher was concerned with productive vocabulary – she wanted the learners to be able to produce the target items readily and intelligibly, whereas the second teacher was more concerned with developing the learner's ability to use the context to infer meanings.

USE OF TRANSLATION

Of course, it is not possible for the learner to guess the meanings of the target word or phrase on every occasion. It may be simply too difficult, or it might take up too much of class time. What are the alternative procedures? The most obvious one is the use of translation. At one time almost all foreign language teaching was done by translation. All expressions in the target language were immediately translated, and new words were usually recorded in a 'vocabulary notebook'. The result of this approach was usually that the target language was very little used in the foreign language lessons – most of the time was taken up with the mother tongue! The students had very little opportunity to practise using the foreign vocabulary in conversation, or even writing, and hardly ever got to the point of thinking in the foreign language.

Many teachers reacted against this by attempting to ban the mother tongue from their classes completely. While this was on the whole a healthy reaction, it is perhaps a bit extreme. As we have seen in our first example, use of the mother tongue, especially at the elementary stage, can save a lot of time, and also, perhaps, reassure the learner in what might be a rather threatening situation.

On the whole, however, translation of vocabulary into the mother tongue should be kept under tight control. From the lower intermediate stage onwards it is better to explain a word (if it cannot be elicited) by using a simple explanation in the target language. Apart from giving the student extra exposure to the target language this technique has another benefit: if on a future occasion he cannot call to mind the target item, *he can always give an explanation*. This is a technique that is in fact often used by native speakers when they cannot think of the best word in a particular situation: they will approximate to it, by giving a synonym or an explanation of it. Students who have been taught by translation techniques often give up if the exact word or phrase does not come to mind, while those who are used to operating in the target language will often have alternative phrasing to fall back on.

4 The Teaching of Vocabulary in Context

Vocabulary is most frequently taught in a spoken or written context, and we have already seen that there are good arguments for this approach. What we are going to do now is look at contexts at various levels, and discuss ways in which they can be exploited for vocabulary teaching purposes. The first two contexts are 'authentic' in the sense that they were originally written with a native-speaker audience in mind.

The first extract is from a magazine for young people called *Look and Learn*:

Nobody who made the climb up the terrible Chilkoot pass in the winter of 1898 ever forgot it. Of all the natural hazards of the trail to Dawson City, this appalling frozen staircase of snow and mud was unquestionably the worst. The foot of the pass was heaped
5 with bodies of mules, pack ponies and sledge dogs that had died in the attempt to reach the top. For weeks on end the snow-covered trail was black with an endless column of men who were making the climb on their own two feet, laden down with their supplies.
10 If a man stopped to catch his breath, the sweat froze to his skin beneath his clothes. If he tried to free the clothes, the skin of his body tore off in strips. With face grotesquely swollen by the biting wind, many a half-blinded man stumbled into a crevasse and was never seen again; and yet the remainder never faltered.
15 They were miners and prospectors driven on through these nightmare conditions by the lure of something for which men had risked their lives since the dawn of history – gold!

As we have seen, the first task is to ensure that the students have a general understanding of the passage. Assuming that they do, what vocabulary might the teacher concentrate on?

The teacher will look for words which the students might not know, but which are fully supported by the context, so that their meaning might be inferred. Words which come into this category are: *hazard/natural hazard; appalling; unquestionably, endless, laden down, catch one's breath, grotesquely, crevasse; prospectors,* and *lure.*

Hazard may be best approached through the immediate context: the Chilkoot pass is an example of a natural danger. It might be approached thus: Was the trail to Dawson City dangerous? (Yes.) Name the worst of the dangerous parts. (The Chilkoot pass.) So what do we mean by saying that the Chilkoot pass was a hazard? (It was dangerous.)

Another useful technique which works for many passages is to list words which are related in meaning. In the passage under consideration we put it to the students that in this passage the writer is trying to give us an impression of how awful the 1898 gold-rush was for the prospectors, and ask: What describing words (adjectives) does the writer use to show us how awful conditions were? We should come up with words like:

> *terrible*   (Chilkoot pass)
> *appalling*   (frozen staircase)
> *nightmare*   (conditions)

and perhaps

> *grotesquely*   (swollen face)

Similarly words which build up the picture of terribly cold conditions can be listed:

> *winter*
> *frozen*   (staircase)
> *snow*
> *snow-covered*   (trail)
> *biting*   (wind)

The last-mentioned word (*biting*) is an example of a metaphoric use of language, the meaning of which can usually be easily inferred. If we ask what sort of things usually bite (e.g. dogs), we can ask the class to guess the meaning of a 'biting wind'.

Difficult words such as *crevasse* and *lure* are perhaps guessable from the context. A man is stumbling along in the snow and suddenly disappears, never to be seen again – what has happened to him? *Lure* is the trickier word of the two since there are two meanings which fit: 'attraction' (roughly the correct meaning) and 'desire'. Perhaps the teacher might consider backtracking to the original meaning of *lure* in the sense of 'bait' to catch someone: Let's look at this word 'lure'. How is it that anglers attract fish? (worms, flies, etc.). So fish are attracted or lured to their deaths by worms and flies. What was it that lured the prospectors to their deaths? (gold). So what is a lure? (something attractive, but perhaps leading to a dangerous trap).

The word *prospectors* allows us to use another useful classroom technique, which at the same time allows us to develop knowledge of word-meaning and also of related forms. What were these men looking for? (Gold.) Yes, they were *prospecting* for gold. So what do we mean when we say that someone is a gold prospector? . . . The students have been given ample information to infer the meaning and also to use the word productively.

The meanings of words such as *unquestionably* (1.4) and *endless* (1.7) are easily inferred from analysing their internal structure. The students' attention can be drawn to the use of *un-* and *-less*, both to give roughly the same meaning: 'without' (unquestionably = without question/endless = without end).

As one last example of a vocabulary item we might like to teach from this passage, there is the expression *catch his breath* in 1.*10*. This is, of course, an example of an idiom. Unlike some idioms, the internal structure of this idiom is fairly 'transparent': in other words, the component words *catch/his/breath* are all fairly common words which retain something of their original meaning when combined in the idiom. The meaning of the phrase is therefore not too difficult to elicit.

We have therefore five categories of expressions in this passage:

(1)   words that can be inferred from context (e.g. *hazard*);
(2)   words in the same semantic field which can be related and discussed together (*terrible/appalling*, etc.);
(3)   words which can be taught through related forms (*prospect/ prospector*);
(4)   words having a common literal sense which are used metaphorically (*biting*); and
(5)   words and idioms that can be interpreted by analysing their internal structure (*unquestionably/catch one's breath*).

At this point, you might like to look back at the passage to see whether there are any other words or expressions which fall into one of these five categories.

Teachers using authentic texts for vocabulary work may often come across texts which lend themselves to a particular kind of vocabulary-development approach. The following passage, for example, lends itself to the discussion of words in the same semantic field. The field will be obvious enough, but what are the relevant words/expressions? (The passage is taken from the 'Behaviour' column of *Time* Magazine, 5 January, 1981.)

Psychologist Jean Piaget vividly remembered an attempt to kidnap him from his baby carriage along the Champs Elysées. He recalled the gathered crowd, the scratches on the face of the heroic nurse who saved him, the policeman's white baton, the
5 assailant running away. However vivid, Piaget's recollections were false. Years later the nurse confessed that she had made up the entire story.

Many social scientists believe that most early childhood memories are dreamlike reconstructions of stories told by
10 parents and friends. Now Elizabeth Loftus, a psychologist at the University of Washington at Seattle, has a sobering message for grown-ups: their memories are almost as unreliable as children's – so encrusted with experiences, desires and suggestions that they often resemble fiction as much as fact. In *Eyewitness*
15 *Testimony*, a book she published a year ago, Loftus made a strong case against the reliability of remembrances of court

witnesses. In her latest work, *Memory*, she indicts human recollections in general.

One problem with memory, says Loftus, is that people do not
20 observe well in the first place. Surprisingly often, people fail a
simple test: picking out the exact copy of a real penny coin in a
group of 15 possible designs. More important, people forget
some facts and 'refabricate' the gaps between the ones they do
remember accurately; they tend to adjust memory to suit their
25 picture of the world.

The passage is, of course, about memory, and the following
related words are found:

> (vividly) remember/remembered
> recalled
> (vivid) recollections
> memory/memories
> (reliability of) remembrances

Also present are expressions connected with the lack of memory,
as it were:

> forget
> false (recollections)
> dreamlike reconstructions
> unreliable (memories)
> fiction
> 'refabricate'
> to adjust memory

Also relevant are the expressions: reliability (of memory);
(remember) accurately; vividly remember; vivid recollections.

Some of these expressions are unusual and more suitable to
receptive rather than active use. Nevertheless, the establishment of
semantic clusters like this, derived from authentic texts, is a useful
way of expanding vocabulary. This is not only because distinctions
and similarities are established between words in the same semantic

field, but also because useful collocations such as *remember accurately*, *vividly remember*, *unreliable memory*, etc. are established.

As with any passage for comprehension, the first task would be to ensure that the students have an overall understanding of the main information in the passage. Only when such overall understanding exists should the student be asked to infer the meaning of individual words. The reader might like to think of five or six questions which might elicit this general understanding.

The main points in the passage would appear to be:

(1)   the incident that happened to Piaget,
(2)   the fact that the story was false,
(3)   the belief among scientists that most childhood memories are false,
(4)   the argument of Loftus that the same applies to adult memories,
(5)   the reason for this being that people don't observe well,
(6)   and that they make up what they don't know.

Once these points have been established, the teacher can turn his attention to the vocabulary of the passage, if this is what he wants to do. (There are of course many other ways in which this passage could be exploited: at the present time we assume that the teacher is interested in vocabulary development.)

The lesson might develop along these lines (*T* = teacher, *P* = pupil):

T: We have said that Piaget remembered an attempt to kidnap him as a baby. Was this a clear memory, or was it a confused one?

P: Confused.

T: Do you think so? What were the things he remembered about the incident?

P: The crowd.

P: The scratches on his nurse's face.

T: Yes. Anything else?

P: The policeman's white baton.

P: Someone running away.

T: Yes, he could remember the assailant, the man who attacked him, running away. Remember we are talking about a baby. Is this a clear memory for a baby?

P: Yes, it is clear.

T: So he seemed to remember clearly. Is there a word in the first line which means 'to remember *clearly*'?

P: *Vividly*.

T: Good. So to remember vividly is to remember in a very clear, lifelike way – almost as if it was happening again in front of you. Does that word come anywhere else in the passage – or a word related to it?

P: Yes – line 5.

T: Yes, line 5 tells us that Piaget's recollections were vivid but false. False means . . .?

P: Not true.

T: So recollections can be vivid but false. There is a word in line 9 which means the same as 'recollections'. Can you find it?

P: Memories.

T: And in line 16, there is a word which means the same as *memories* or *recollections*. Can you find it?

P: Remembrances.

T: Very good. So we have these three words which mean more or less the same thing. (Writes *recollections*, *memories*, *remembrances*, on the blackboard). The most common one is *memories*. Yes. There's also another word that is used, in the first paragraph, that means the same as *remembered*. Can you find it?

P: *Recalled*.

T: Good. So we have *remembered* and *recalled*. (Writes these words on b/b.) Now. Can you remind me again about what the social scientists said about early childhood memories?

P: Reconstructions.

T: Yes, can you say the whole thing?

P: They are 'dreamlike reconstructions of stories told by

parents and friends'.

T: So where do the children get their memories from?

P: From dreams.

T: Yes, we'll come to the dream bit in a minute. The children are really too young to remember, aren't they? Piaget was only a baby. Where do they hear the stories they make into memories? Whom do they hear them from?

P: From parents and friends.

T: And we are told that the memories are 'reconstructions' of these stories. What does that mean?

P: They are made up from the stories they heard.

T: So *to reconstruct* means ...?

P: To make up.

T: From ...?

P: The stories.

T: Yes, in this case. Generally, it means to make up something from something else. Look at line *23*. Do you see a word there that is like *reconstruct*.

P: Refabricate?

T: Refabricate. Refabricate. Right. Do you think it means something the same as *reconstruct*, *make up*? Look at the sentence.

P: Yes.

T: Good. Read me the bit from 'people' to 'accurately', but use *make up* instead of *refabricate*.

P: 'People forget some facts and make up the gaps between the ones they do remember accurately.'

T: Does that make good sense?

P: Yes.

T: Yes, very good. So *to reconstruct*, *to make up something from something else* and *to refabricate* all seem to mean more or less the same thing. (Writes the three expressions on the b/b.)

The lesson is, of course, not finished yet but perhaps enough of it has been shown to illustrate the teacher's general approach. What techniques were used by the teacher to exploit the vocabulary of this passage? See if you can find specific examples of these techniques in operation. Are there any other techniques the teacher might have used to teach these vocabulary items? Are there any teaching points which you would have liked to give some attention to? The teacher's blackboard presentation at the end of the lesson is shown in Figure 4.1.

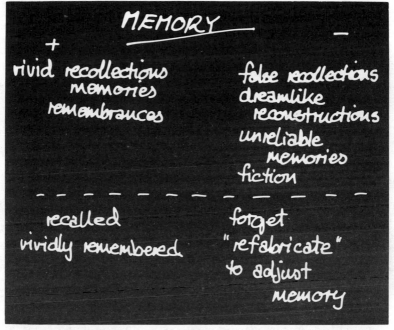

Fig. 4.1   Final blackboard presentation for lesson on semantic clusters (see pp. 52 to 57)

The sort of techniques we have been describing need not be applied only to content words. The teacher may wish, for example, to direct the learners' attention to what are sometimes called discourse markers or semantic markers. These are words which related to the structure of a context and show how statements (propositions) relate to each other. In the passage which follows, some examples of these markers occur.

The need for money originates from the fact that different people in society produce different things. *This means that* people depend on each other for goods and services. *Let us take the case of* a farmer who produces more food than he requires and a carpenter who lives by selling the tables and chairs that he has made. *It will be obvious* that unless some means of exchange is found, the farmer will not be able to get rid of his surplus food and the carpenter will starve! *Clearly*, the simplest means of exchange will be for them to use barter – *in other words*, to exchange a certain amount of one kind of goods (let's say flour) for a certain amount of another (tables or chairs, in this case).

Obviously, barter can work only in a very simple society. In an advanced society one cannot go around carrying things in the hope that we can exchange them for the things we need.

So we need something which will stand for the goods and services that we want to exchange. *Hence* the origin of money. *It follows* that anything can act as money or currency, provided that all the people using it agree on its value. We are not surprised to find, *therefore*, the use of very many different kinds of money at one time or another. Examples of 'currencies' that have been used in the past are cowrie shells, coconuts, whales' teeth and salt. *As one might expect*, things used as money have certain qualities, *namely* that they should be firstly convenient, secondly durable (that is, long lasting) and lastly of some rarity value. *Thus* we would *not* expect large stones to be used as money (because they are too inconvenient), or fruits or plants (because they go bad eventually), nor pebbles (because they are too common). *Nevertheless*, it is interesting to note that these rules do not work all the time. *To take one good example*, there is an island in the Pacific Ocean where the natives used large stone wheels as currency; sometimes these wheels were as big as twelve feet across! They were sometimes stored outside a man's house as a sign of his wealth.

(M. J. Wallace, Study Skills in English)

After the passage has been discussed, students might be asked to find words and phrases which show:

cause and effect;
that an example is being introduced;
that the meaning of something is to be explained;
that something is obvious;
that one idea is being opposed to another.

The examples of discourse markers can then be grouped together by category for blackboard presentation.

In this chapter the treatment of vocabulary in context has been featured, but this should not leave a false impression. A lot of vocabulary work will be done incidentally as it arises naturally out of the discussion of the meaning of the passage. There is something to be said for the systematic presentation of vocabulary, especially on the blackboard (as we shall see later) but this does not mean that there should always, or even most times, be a separate section of the lesson plan labelled 'vocabulary work'. Indeed many textbooks do the teacher a disservice by having a list of words and phrases listed separately under 'vocabulary', which tempts the teacher to deal with them separately and not as they arise naturally from the lesson.

In general the teacher should be wary of lists of words or phrases to be explained. He should ask himself if it is not possible to have these words/phrases explained by the students as they arise naturally from the text, rather than as something separate from the total meaning of the passage. The total meaning must always be of the prime importance. We have seen how words or phrases can often be related to one another in a meaningful way, and the teacher should be on the look-out for opportunities to do this, when it fits in with the overall aim of the lesson.

By and large, therefore, it is safer for the teacher to devise his own vocabulary questions than to follow the textbook. This usually makes lessons livelier and more interesting, especially as all too many textbooks seem to be concerned with *testing* vocabulary rather than *teaching* it. Many textbooks, for example, make extensive use of multiple-choice questions. These can be excellent for testing vocabulary, but are not necessarily the best way of teaching it. As we have seen, good vocabulary teaching requires a flexible, oral approach which leads the students by easy stages to a reasonable guess as to the meaning of the target item.

If you ask a student to explain the meaning of a word or phrase, make sure that what you are asking can be done within the student's language resources. Even for native speakers, it is possible to *understand* what a phrase means without being able to *explain* it, which is essentially a productive exercise. For example, one book of comprehension exercises for EFL which has been widely used, asks students to explain the meaning of the word 'worse' and the phrase 'one can do as one likes' as they are used in the passage! The expressions themselves are, of course, simple: but to explain them in simpler language is virtually impossible.

Another common technique is for the teacher simply to ask 'Does anyone know the meaning of this word?' This is a legitimate question which can save a lot of time. If over-used, however, it can make the less able students lazy (they can rely on X and Y to do the work), and furthermore it encourages the idea that vocabulary is something that you either know (especially if you happen to be X or Y) or don't know. It is often good strategy to find out which students know (or think they know) the meaning, then to help the others guess the meaning, checking with the first group that the 'discovered' meaning was what they had in mind, thus giving the bright students their moment of glory.

A useful technique, which cuts out the problem of the students having to produce an explanation, is to provide the students with the *meaning* and then to ask them to find the word or phrase: 'There is a word in the passage we've just read which means "danger" – can you find it?' If the students are still in difficulty, the teacher can focus in on the target item as finely as is necessary: 'It's in the first paragraph ... the second sentence ...' (etc.).

STORING AND MEMORIZING VOCABULARY

It happens very often that vocabulary is *taught* in context, but is not *stored* and *memorized* in context, and it is to this important point that we turn now.

Foreign learners arc very fond of noting down new vocabulary items as they come across them. This enthusiasm is very heartening for the teacher, but his enthusiasm is liable to wane when he looks at the notes that they have been taking. They are often just a chaotic jumble of isolated words and phrases, often collected in different notebooks, hopeless from the point of view of either *retrieval* or *memorization*. Let us look at each of these in turn.

Retrieval
Presumably one of the reasons for noting down a word or phrase in the target language is that one thinks one may have need of it later. But if it is buried among hundreds of other miscellaneous words and phrases, how is it to be found when it is needed?

Memorization
Usually the learner puts the target word or phrase down with its mother tongue equivalent or, less frequently, an explanation in English. If he is conscientious he will then attempt to memorize the target word and its translation, usually simply by repeating it over and over again. This is obviously a somewhat boring and inefficient method of learning vocabulary.

It can be assumed that noting new vocabulary is not something which, generally speaking, the teacher would wish to discourage. That being so, how could it be made more efficient?

One method that has been advocated is the use of vocabulary cards as a preferable alternative to the vocabulary notebook (see Nation, 1980, and Sandosham, 1980). The most basic form of vocabulary card has the target word/phrase on one side and the translation or explanation on the other. The advantages of cards for retrieval are obvious, since they can be arranged alphabetically either by target word or translation, or they can be arranged/rearranged by topic. The latter would be very useful for the learner when, say, writing a composition. As Linda Sandosham points out, the vocabulary cards then become a kind of 'word-bank' on which the learner draws according to his vocabulary needs.

The cards should help memorization also, since vocabulary learning then becomes a kind of contest which the learner plays against himself: Can I guess what's one the other side of this card? Some learners simply use pieces of paper folded in three: target word/translation/example sentence.

Another technique which can be very effective when learning the basic vocabulary of a new language is to attempt to make some sort of 'meaning bridge' between the target word and its L1 translation. It does not matter how far-fetched or ridiculous the 'bridge' is: in fact, some would say that the more grotesque it is, the better for memorization. It helps if the bridge can be clearly visualized in the learner's mind.

To illustrate this technique, let us take the case of an English speaker attempting to learn the numerals in a very different, unrelated language: Turkish, perhaps. The equivalents for 1–5 are: one – bir; two – iki; three – üç; four – dört; five – beş. The first word sounds like 'beer', so the learner might think of ordering *one* very large foaming *beer*. The second word (*iki*) contains *two* 'eyes', so that might be the connection there. The third word (*üç*) has three 'extra marks' (two dots and the cedilla under the letter *c*). There is also a progression: one 'mark' for *bir*, two for *iki* and three for *üç*. The fourth word (*dört*) is pronounced something like 'dirt', and *four* rhymes with 'door', so the learner might think of an old *door* very heavily encrusted with *dirt*. Similarly, *five* rhymes with *hive*, and the word *beş* looks rather similar to the word *bees* (although it is pronounced very differently), so we have the 'bridge': five – hive – bees – beş.

This process might strike some readers as rather laborious, if not downright silly. Nevertheless, it is a well-tried technique used by professional 'memory-men', and there is some evidence that this and similar techniques can be also effectively used in learning foreign languages (for an interesting review of this topic see Meara, 1981). At the very least, it is a means of making the learner think actively about what he is trying to remember, instead of the mindless repetition which often passes for vocabulary 'learning'. It may be that the effort to make the link between the target word and the translation may be of more value than the link itself.

At the elementary level, learners can be encouraged to make their own picture dictionaries, using drawings instead of L1 translations. An interesting group activity might be making posters related to a theme for the classroom wall: 'Motor cars' perhaps, or 'In the kitchen'. The posters would contain magazine cut-outs with target language equivalents.

If the students do use traditional vocabulary notebooks, then the orderly presentation of vocabulary on the blackboard (as in Figure 4.1) may be very helpful to them. Some of the exercises which will be mentioned in the next two chapters which draw different vocabulary items together may also be helpful in this respect: see, for example, Figure 5.1 on p. 81 and Figure 6.1 on p. 91.

None of this, of course, contradicts what has been said about the long-term benefits of learning vocabulary in context, in the ways that have been described. Students will want to store vocabulary and will have to memorize it, and we should help them in any way we can.

5 Exercises for Vocabulary Development (1)

The point has been made repeatedly so far that the best way of developing one's vocabulary in a foreign language is to encounter it in situations and contexts which are as authentic as possible, without causing the learner to be overwhelmed and frustrated by the quantity and/or difficulty of the new material. In this chapter and the next, however, we shall be looking at vocabulary development exercises which are to a greater or lesser extent removed from the kind of situational or contextual learning that we have had in mind so far.

These exercises can be used for various purposes. First, the teacher can look at them from the point of view of *expanding his or her range of techniques* when involved in vocabulary teaching from a context or in a situation. Many of the approaches discussed here may be introduced in an *ad hoc* way, as opportunity arises, to exploit some aspect of the language that the learner is currently encountering.

Secondly, the exercises can be used to *focus on some aspect of vocabulary learning*: for example, by bringing together some points about vocabulary which may have been dealt with so far in a rather random or unsystematic way. In this connection, one may think of exercises in word-roots, language variety (e.g. legal, medical, scientific), cohesion, and so on.

Thirdly, some aspects of vocabulary (but not all) can be developed in an *autonomous* or *semi-autonomous* way, i.e. more or less independently of the teacher. Provided that the student is able to correct his answers, vocabulary is one of those areas of language-learning where a well-motivated learner can make giant strides on his own if he is given the right kind of material to work on, and vocabulary development exercises can have a role to play here.

Fourthly, some of the exercises can also be used as *tests*. Vocabulary testing is another subject which will be dealt with in detail later (Chapter 7): at this point it is perhaps sufficient to point out that many of the so-called 'vocabulary exercises' found in textbooks and courses are, in fact, tests. The purpose of a vocabulary exercise is *to develop the learner's command of target language vocabulary*, not simply to find out whether she/he knows a particular item of vocabulary or not. However, a close relationship exists between tests and exercises, since many exercises can be made into tests and vice versa.

WORD-MEANING EXERCISES

In this chapter, the exercises we shall be looking at may all be grouped together under the rather vague heading of 'word-meaning', subdivided into: *inference exercises, synonym/antonym exercises, semantic field exercises*, and *definition and dictionary exercises*.

INFERENCE EXERCISES

One useful type of inference exercise is to use short contexts to show learners the different ways in which the meaning of an unknown word (which we shall call the 'target word') can be inferred from its context. In the following example *furniture* is the target word:

All the *furniture* had been completely removed so that not a single table or chair was to be seen.

Here the learner should be able to guess the meaning of *furniture*, from the **examples** of furniture which are mentioned. But what if the learner already happens to know the meaning of *furniture*? Is the example wasted? Not necessarily, perhaps, if we can ask him how he would have been able to guess the meaning of *furniture* anyway.

This consideration, however, has led some writers (Alderson and

Alvarez, 1978) to suggest that nonsense words should be used in such exercises, rather than real words. In that way, the learner (and the teacher) can concentrate on the techniques of inference rather than the meaning of any particular word.

Another solution is simply to leave a blank, but this may deprive the learner of useful clues such as a plural form or a past tense form (indicating a verb).

A compromise solution might be to have a particular English word in mind, but to use some agreed formula such as the form *targetword* wherever the 'unknown' word is to be guessed. So the example we have been looking at would read:

All the *targetword* had been completely removed so that not a single table or chair was to be seen.

There are three possible ways of answering this, all of which are acceptable:

(1)   The learner can substitute the English word *furniture*, if he happens to know it.
(2)   In a class where all the students speak the same language, which the teacher understands, then the mother-tongue equivalent may be given. This shows that the student has correctly inferred the meaning of *targetword* (i.e. furniture in this case). If the teacher decides it is useful (although the students will probably demand it anyway), the English word can be given;
(3)   the student may attempt some kind of definition of *targetword* which will allow the teacher to decide whether he has grasped its meaning.

In all these cases, a most useful follow-up is for the student to explain *how* he has inferred the meaning of the word: this is probably more important in the long run than whether he has got the particular example right or wrong.

Some examples of different types of short-context inference exercises follow – the heading in block capitals indicates the type of inference clue given.

(1) DEFINITION. Many animals live only by killing other animals and eating them: they are called *targetword* animals. (Carnivorous/predatory, etc. This is the simplest type of inference, since the definition is simply given.)

(2) HYPONYM/HEADWORD. The museum contained almost every type of *targetword*: cars, buses, trams, and even old carriages and coaches. (Vehicle. This word is being used here as a *hyponym*, i.e. it includes all the other terms which are listed. A simpler term for *hyponym* would be 'headword'.)

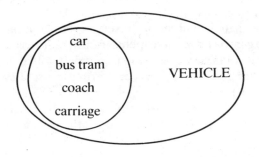

(3) CO—HYPONYM/EXAMPLE. As we wandered through the market, we were amazed at the quantity and variety of fruit on display. One stall contained only oranges, another lemons, another apples of various kinds and so it went on: grapes, *targetwords*, melons, grapefruit ... (Obviously, some kind of fruit, but we do not have enough information to specify which kind. All the examples of *fruit* [which is, of course, a hyponym] are *co-hyponyms*: so the words oranges, lemons, apples, grapes, melons, grapefruit are co-hyponyms of the general term *fruit*; and the unknown term must be a co-hyponym of *fruit* also. A simpler term to use with learners would be 'example'.)

(4) CHARACTERISTIC OR QUALITY. (a) The *targetword* was far too large for our needs: its two floors contained four public rooms and six bedrooms, and the garden extended for almost an acre. (Obviously a house of some kind; perhaps a villa: mention of two floors seems to exclude bungalow, and the mention of a garden

makes flat unlikely. This kind of example, can lead into an interesting discussion of the characteristics of different kinds of houses.)

(b)   There was no doubting his physical *targetword*: on several occasions he fought off several of the enemy singlehanded. (Courage or bravery, 'singlehanded' is also a word worth discussing, but is probably best dealt with by analysing its structure, as will be discussed in the next chapter.)

(5)   SYNONYM.   (a)   We had never seen such a large cave: it was simply *targetword*. (Enormous, huge, etc. Obviously the unknown word is a synonym for 'very large'.)

(b)   Many people had serious reservations about the plan. One common *targetword* was the expense of it. (? Criticism. This is an example of a common device, where a writer will avoid using the same word for stylistic reasons, preferring to use a synonym, or near-synonym.)

(6)   ANTONYM.   Our last employer was extremely mean, but our present employer, Mr Jones, is one of the most *targetword* men it has been my pleasure to meet. (Generous. The word *but*, with *pleasure*, indicates contrast.)

(7)   GENERAL KNOWLEDGE.   The hotel has every facility. At the top of it there is even a *targetword* which will take you straight to and from the airport if you are in a hurry. (Helicopter. The ability to guess this word and/or its meaning depends to some extent on the student's background knowledge.)

There is a more advanced and elaborate type of follow-up to this kind of exercise where a number of 'unknown' words are located in one passage. The learner is asked not to define the target words, but to indicate which words or phrases are helpful in inferring the meaning. Again, the unknown words may be real or invented.

The country of Norway, seen in isolation from its eastern neighbour Sweden, looks like a great, pre-historic, *fossilized* human hand stretching down from the Arctic towards Denmark and Britain. It is a right hand, palm downwards to the ocean, a
5 stubby thumb towards the east clenched into the *forefinger*. Up the crack between thumb and forefinger lies Oslo, its capital.

To the north the fractured forearm bones stretch up to Tromso
and Hammerfest, deep in the Arctic, so *narrow* that in places
there are only forty miles from the sea to the Swedish border.
10 On a relief map the hand looks as if it has been smashed by some
gigantic hammer of the gods, *splintering* bones and knuckles into
thousands of particles. Nowhere is this *breakage* more marked
than along the west coast, where the chopping edge of the hand
would be.
15 Here the land is shattered into a thousand fragments and
between the *shards* the sea has flowed in to form a million *creeks*,
gullies, bays and gorges; winding narrow defiles where the
mountains fall sheer to glittering water. These are the *fjords*, and
it was from the headwaters of these that a race of men came out
20 1500 years ago who were the best sailors ever to set *keel* to the
water or sail to the wind. Before their age was over they had
sailed to Greenland and America, conquered Ireland, settled
Britain and Normandy, hunted to Spain and Morocco and *navigated* from the Mediterranean to Iceland. They were the
25 Vikings, and their descendants still live and fish along the fjords
of Norway.

(Frederick Forsyth: *The Devil's Alternative*)

Target word	Helpful words or phrases
1 fossilized	....
	....
2 forefinger	....
	....
3 narrow	....
	....
4 splintering	....
	....
5 breakage	....

6 shards

....

....

7 creeks

....

....

8 fjords

....

....

9 keel

....

....

10 navigated

....

....

SYNONYM AND ANTONYM EXERCISES

One of the problems about the use of synonym and antonym exercises is that some linguists wonder whether there is really such a thing as a 'true synonym' or 'true antonym' in a strict interpretation of those words. For example, if we take 'synonym' to mean one word which means exactly the same as another in all possible contexts, we shall have great difficulty in finding a synonym in these circumstances. Sometimes the problem lies in denotation, i.e. the words refer to slightly different things, though some of the meanings may overlap. Let us look, for example, at the words *border* and *frontier*. These words may be regarded as synonyms in the sense that they both refer to the boundary that exists between one country and another. Of course each of these words also has many senses which the other does not normally have. For example, a design on a cushion may have a *border* – it certainly wouldn't have a *frontier*! But even in the sense that they have in common (boundary between one country and another), there is a difference in emphasis: *frontier* has connotations of danger or hostility: so that, in the United States, for example, the limit of what had been colonized or settled was called the *frontier*, and one speaks of the 'frontier spirit', i.e. willingness to face danger or discomfort while settling a new area. One would not call the boundary between England and Scotland a *frontier*, although there is a *border* between these two countries.

The example given with reference to the United States also reminds us that *frontier* often has the idea of a boundary that changes and advances, whereas the *border* may be more fixed. This is extended metaphorically into such uses as the *frontiers* of medicine, or the *frontiers* of science, i.e. the outermost limits of what is known about these areas.

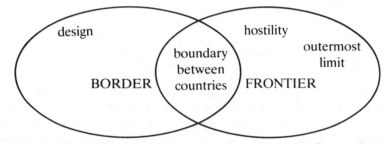

A more obvious example of words which are synonyms in many contexts is *big* and *large*. So we can say *I need a big envelope*, or *I need a large envelope*. On the other hand, *big* tends to be more colloquial and can be used in contexts like, '*What a big boy you are!*' where *large* would sound quite inappropriate. There are also, of course, idiomatic phrases where the two words are not interchangeable, such as in the expression *by and large* (in the sense of 'on the whole' or 'for the most part'). Another distinction is in forms derived from these words, such as the adverb *largely*: there is no one-word equivalent to be derived from *big*. A similar example is *little* and *small*: I can refer to a *child* as a *small child* or a *little child*, but if I want to refer to a child who is *even smaller* than the first one, I can only use *small*. The comparative of *little* (*less*) cannot be used in this way.

Sometimes synonyms will only 'work one way'.

Look at this sentence:

Is John old enough to drive a vehicle?

If we ask a student to give a synonym for *vehicle* in this sentence, he might suggest *car*, which might be acceptable. But it should be clear that *car* is acceptable only as a *type* of vehicle: all cars are vehicles, but not all vehicles are cars (they might be lorries, for example).

So here we have a relationship:

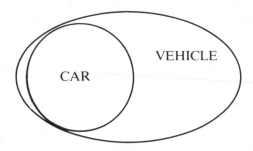

This does not mean of course that *vehicle* can always be used instead of car: for one thing, *vehicle* is a far more formal word. It would sound absurd to say, 'I'll just go round and put my vehicle into the garage' (unless, of course, one were deliberately trying to be funny).

So we can see that words which are generally thought to be synonyms may be quite different either with respect to different aspects of their 'meaning' (i.e. denotation), or the contexts in which they may be used, or the words that they may collocate with.

There does not, therefore, appear to be a lot of sense in encouraging students to think in terms of synonyms as such. In general, we are concerned with meaning. For example, if the word *enthusiast* occurs in a passage and we wish to explore its meaning, it seems more sensible to accept a definition or explanation (such as 'this means a person who shows a very keen interest in something') rather than to insist on a one-word equivalent (e.g. 'fanatic') which does not have exactly the same meaning anyway. (*Fanatic* usually has unfavourable connotations, which *enthusiast* does not normally have).

Possibly of more use to the learner are exercises which explore the *differences* between words with overlapping meanings. Some example exercises are listed below.

Area of reference exercise
Match the following words with the area of reference in which they are most commonly used. You can use a dictionary to help you.

Word		*Area of reference*	
1	partner	A	war
2	colleague	B	friendship
3	ally	C	business, firm
4	accomplice	D	profession
5	comrade	E	crime

Level of formality exercise
Here are some words with similar meanings: *pal, mate, associate, companion, buddy, friend.* Write them into the boxes according to their level of formality. You may use a dictionary.

Formal	*Neutral*	*Informal*

Collocation exercise
Here are some verbs: cut (down/up/off), hew (down), hack (at), chop (down/off), carve (up), slit (open). Which of them would normally be used with the nouns or noun-phrases which are listed below?

Verb	*Noun/noun phrase*
_____	a tree
_____	roast meat

_____   an envelope

_____   a door

_____   one's initials (e.g. on a tree)

_____   wood (for firewood)

_____   wood (to make a design)

_____   a skirt

_____   coal

_____   a finger

_____   a branch of a tree

_____   one's wrist

_____   a wooden barrier

Scale exercise

Arrange the following words in three groups, in ascending order. In the first set, for example, *big* would be placed in the first group, *spacious* in the second group and *immense* in the third group; similarly, in the second set, *little* would be in the first group, *tiny* in the second group, and *microscopic* in the third group.

(1) immense, big, enormous, large, gigantic, spacious, colossal, extensive.
(2) little, tiny, microscopic, small, minute, infinitesimal, diminutive.
(3) distinguished, famous, well-known, illustrious, renowned.
(4) mansion, house, palace, castle, cottage, cabin, hut.
(5) gale, breeze, storm, hurricane, wind. (When you have finished this set, check up the *Beaufort scale* in an encyclopaedia.)

Specific/general exercise

Some words are more specific or particular and others arc more general, although they may refer to the same things. So, for example, *tulip* is more specific than *flower*, since a tulip is a particular kind of flower, but *flower* is more specific than *plant*, since *plant* also includes other growing things such as *bush* or *vegetable*. In the following exercise, see if you can find words to fill in the blanks. If you get stuck, use a dictionary or (if you have one) a thesaurus.

Specific		*General*
tulip	flower	plant
1 cow	....	....
2 coupé/limousine/ saloon	....	....
3 chisel/hammer	....	....
4 novel (noun)	....	....
5 novelist	....	....
6 jeans	....	....
7 pineapple	....	....
8 whisky	....	....
9 scream (noun)	....	....
10 race (verb)	....	....

Attitude exercise

Sometimes people show their attitude to something or someone by their choice of word. So a person who is careful with money may be described as either *frugal* (if you approve) or *miserly* (if you disapprove). After each of the following words put (+) if you think the word is usually approving, (−) if it is usually disapproving, and (=) if you think it is neutral. The first three are done for you:

frugal (+), miserly (−), careful (=); famous (   ), notorious (   );
extravagant (   ), generous (   ); strict (   ), severe (   );
obstinate (   ), resolute (   ); inactive (   ), lazy (   ), tired (   ),
sleepy (   ); bright (   ), gaudy (   ); self-respect (   ),
snobbery (   ); rashness (   ), courage (   ); advertise (   ),
boast (   ), brag (   ).

We have already discussed some of the problems of whether or not there is really such a thing as a 'true synonym'. The same problem also arises in discussing 'antonyms' (opposites). It is very difficult to think of an antonym unless we have some particular context in mind. For example, if someone asked us for the opposite of *married*, we might suggest *single*; but there is also *divorced* or even *separated*. Which particular 'opposite' is appropriate will depend upon the speaker's frame of reference, i.e. the speaker may be contrasting married people with single people, or he may be contrasting those who are still married with those who have been divorced. Similarly, is the antonym of *old* the word *new* or the word *young*? It depends on whether we are talking about cars (*new*) or people (*young*). (See Nilsen and Nilsen, 1975).

Some opposites spring easily to mind for cultural reasons or because of the way in which the language works. So if we ask someone to give us the opposite of *white* he will probably say *black*. (Unless, of course, he is thinking of wines, in which case he will probably say *red*!). But if we ask him to give us the opposite of *purple* or *brown* he will probably hesitate, and may want to consult a colour chart before committing himself. The reason for this, of course, is that the terms *black* and *white* are often used contrastively, whereas other colours are not used contrastively so often.

A special type of opposite which sometimes causes problems to learners are those with reciprocal meanings (see p. 20), i.e. they are, as it were, 'mirror images' of each other. Good examples are the reciprocal antonyms *lend* and *borrow*: if A *lends* £20 to B, then B *borrows* £20 from A. We can represent it like this:

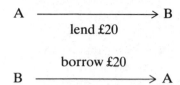

Similarly, if A is B's *parent*, then B is A's *child*. In all of these, one of the terms necessarily implies the other: if A has lent something to B, then B must have borrowed something from A. Other examples of reciprocal antonyms are *employer/employee* and *husband/wife*.

As with synonyms, therefore, antonym exercises should not lead students to think that words normally have one opposite, but rather to make them aware of the network of relationships which can exist between words. Some possible exercises follow.

Antonyms in brief contexts
In the following sentences, supply a word which is the opposite of the word underlined.

(1)   I have <u>lent</u> John another £10: that is the third time he has

_____ money from me this month.

(2)   I get on well with my <u>uncle</u> Jim, and I think I am his favourite

_____.

(3)   Although he was thought to be rather <u>dull</u> at school, he later

became a _____ scholar.

(4)   When   the   general   <u>commands</u>,   the   soldiers   should

_____.

(5)   We'll <u>set</u> the table if you would _____ it when the

meal is finished.

(to the reader: which of the above pairs of antonyms would you say were *reciprocal antonyms*?)

Antonyms formed by using prefixes
In English there are many prefixes that can be used to give the meaning, 'not ...' (e.g. *un*fair, *non*-smoking compartment, etc). One such prefix is **in**——, which is often used with learned words from Latin or French. Before the letter L, *in*- becomes *il*-; before M, B and P, *in*- becomes *im*-; before R, *in*- becomes *ir*-. Fill in the blanks with a word beginning with *in*-, *il*-, *im*-, or *ir*-, which can be opposite of the word in the first column.

Word	*Opposite*
elegant	_____
possible	_____
legal	_____
regular	_____
convenient	_____
probable	_____
sensitive	_____
moral	_____

literate _____

relevant _____

Do you know any other words formed in this way? If you are not sure of the meanings of any of these words, check them up in your dictionary.

SEMANTIC FIELD EXERCISES

If words are in the same semantic field, then they are in the same related area of meaning. This section obviously overlaps with the previous one: both are involved with forming relationships between words in the same general area of meaning. Some sample activities follow.

Listing relationships
A number of related words are listed and their relationship discussed. For example, the class may be asked to pool all the terms they know connected with *family relationships*, yielding vocabulary such as *mother, father, parent, child, son, daughter, cousin, uncle, niece, nephew, in-law,* etc. A family tree can be discussed (m. = married):

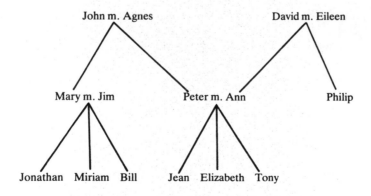

(1)   Jonathan is Peter's _____.

(2)   Peter is Jonathan's _____.

(3)   Jonathan and Bill are _____.

(4)   Miriam and Jean are _____.

(5)   Eileen is Peter's _____.

(Pair work: work out the relationships of other people in the family tree to one another.)

Display with vocabulary key
Look at the drawing of the front view of a car (see Figure 5.1). The twelve parts of the car that are numbered there are also listed below. Put the correct number opposite each item in the list. If there are any terms that you are unfamiliar with, check them up in your dictionary. (*Br.* = British term; *Am.* = American term.)

Term	*Number in drawing*
(a) steering wheel	....
(b) radiator grille	....
(c) bumper (*Br.*)/fender (*Am.*)	....
(d) sidelight	....
(e) bonnet (*Br.*)/hood (*Am.*)	....
(f) indicator light	....
(g) wing-mirror	....
(h) numberplate	....

(i)   windscreen wiper (*Br.*)/
      windshield wiper (*Am.*)   ....

(j)   headlight/headlamp   ....

(k)   windscreen (*Br.*)/windshield (*Am.*)   ....

(l)   rear-view mirror   ....

What other parts of a car do you know? Make a drawing (or some drawings) to show where they are.

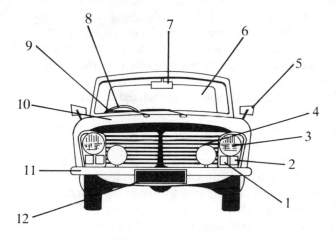

Fig. 5.1

Arranging hierarchies in order
(If students have come across some terms in a hierarchy, it may be useful for the terms to be arranged in order, and the hierarchy made [reasonably] complete. Some examples follow).

Rearrange the following in order starting with the largest, most senior, etc.:

Measure of capacity: quart, fluid ounce, pint, gill, gallon.
Army organization: regiment, platoon, army, battalion, company.
Royal Navy ranks: Commander, Able Seaman, Petty Officer, Admiral, Commodore, Lieutenant, Captain.

The same sort of 'tidying up' process can be applied to other sets of words, e.g. days of the week, months of the year, numbers, fractions, and so on.

DICTIONARY WORK

It has already been stressed that overdependence on the dictionary is a fault is to be avoided. Nevertheless it is obvious that the dictionary can be an extremely useful learning resource, especially as it makes the learner more independent of the teacher. There is hardly any aspect of vocabulary work that the dictionary is not relevant to.

The exercises which follow are related to teaching students the proper use of the dictionary. Bilingual dictionaries are fairly straightforward to use, but there is a lot to be said for the use of monolingual dictionaries, from the point of view of encouraging students to think in the target language. There is now a choice of good monolingual dictionaries available at various levels of difficulty, and specially written for the foreign learner.

The most basic skill in using a dictionary is to find the word or expression one is looking up. A standard exercise for beginners is rearranging words which are out of alphabetical order. Another useful exercise is finding derived forms under another headword, e.g. *pliancy* may be found under *pliant*, or idioms under a headword, e.g. *in the nick of time* may be listed under *nick*.

Another basic use of the dictionary is to find out pronunciation. Most good dictionaries now use the International Phonetic Alphabet (IPA), or a variant of it, to indicate pronunciation. Students should familiarize themselves with it at some stage in their studies. A possible pair-work exercise is where students copy down the phonetic equivalent of some words from the dictionary, which they exchange with their neighbours and then try to reconstruct the normal written forms of the words.

Another pronunciation exercise is to give students lists of words where the English sound system can be confusing, e.g. words ending in *-ough*, such as *cough* or *tough*.

Example: The letters *th* in English usually have two pronounciations, that is either /Ɵ/ or /ð/. Using your dictionary where necessary, put these words into two columns, according to whether they have the sound /Ɵ/ or /ð/:

bath	theft
bathe	through
then	gather
theory	mathematics

Students should also be aware that dictionaries can help them with spelling problems. This can be a trickier procedure than checking pronunciation, because if one is using a monolingual dictionary, it means that one has to be familiar with the various sound-symbol possibilities in English.

The simplest exercises relate to checking on the tricky *endings* of some English words, such as those ending in *-able/-ible*, *-ant/-ent*, etc. One possibility is to give the students a list of such words, some wrongly spelled and some correctly spelled. One might feel uneasy, however, about giving wrong examples in this area, where the learner is so prone to confusion anyway. A better alternative is to use a dictation exercise, where the target word (e.g. *independent*) is read out to the class in a brief context: 'Ghana became an independent republic within the Commonwealth in 1960. Spell *independent*'.

'A person who goes to another country in order to settle there is called an immigrant. Spell *immigrant*.'

After doing perhaps ten such words, students can then use their dictionaries to check their spelling of the target words. Other tricky spelling areas are words involving doubled consonants (e.g.

accommodation) and *e* + *i*/*i* + *e* spellings with the sound /i:/. Any other similar problems raised by the students can be checked up and discussed. It should be remembered, of course, that dictation is not generally considered to be a good method of introducing new vocabulary. Target words for dictation should be words which the students have probably already met in some other context.

Students should realize that the dictionary can also give them⋅ useful grammatical information, sometimes in a more accessible form than a standard reference grammar. They can therefore be given exercises which show them what kind of grammatical information they are likely to find in a dictionary: past tense, past participle and present participle forms; irregular plurals and comparatives or superlatives; and so on.

Examples: (1)   Check up the following past tense forms in your dictionary and note which verbs they came from: *bought, brought, understood, caught, lay.*

(2)   Use your dictionary to find out the present participle (or *-ing* form) of the following verbs: travel, hop, brag, mail, exceed, rob. (This can be followed by a discussion of the rules for doubling consonants in either American English or British English, or both.)

The most important use of the dictionary is to find out the meaning of words, and here the problem is that the learner has to choose the meaning appropriate to a given context when several meanings are defined. The most obvious exercise in this area is also the most useful and valid one. This is simply to take a passage and, after discussing its general sense, to give the students a list of words from it, the meanings of which have to be found from the dictionary. (Words should be chosen which have several meanings.) Students have to write out the correct appropriate definition or (if that is too time-consuming) simply to note the number of the appropriate definition. Answers can then be compared, either in group or class work.

The best dictionaries (although this is still probably more true of monolingual than bilingual dictionaries) contain 'encyclopaedic' information which can be a very useful teaching aid. Thus some dictionaries have useful picture displays of musical instruments, parts of the human body, kinds of animals, stages in the life of an insect, themes (such as camping) and so on, which can be very useful for vocabulary and/or composition work. This is especially true of the picture dictionaries for beginners. These useful dictionaries may take the form of illustrated scenes, usually in colour, covering such topics as 'the human body' or 'the kitchen'. The items illustrated are related to word-lists below the pictures. A word-index at the back may give the pronunciation, and show where the word is illustrated.

6   Exercises for Vocabulary Development (2)

The exercises in this chapter relate more to the structural and contextual aspects of vocabulary development, although it is impossible (and, as we have seen, undesirable) to separate these aspects from the 'meaning' aspect which was the main topic of the last chapter. The distinction is therefore purely one of convenience, and some exercises will appear in this chapter which might just as well have appeared in the last one, and vice versa. The exercises in this chapter will be grouped under the following headings: *word structure, collocation, cohesion*, and *variety*. The teaching of idioms and multi-word verbs, which are special aspects of collocation, will be dealt with separately in the next chapter.

WORD—STRUCTURE EXERCISES

It has already been noted that a knowledge of word-structure is one of the most effective ways of expanding vocabulary, and is of great use in inferring word-meaning. One of the most useful aspects of word-structure is the very common use of *prefixes* and *suffixes* in English. Indeed, there are so many of these that they really ought to be categorized in some way for teaching purposes. In some reference books, prefixes/suffixes are categorized according to their source (usually from Greek, Latin or English) but this does not seem to be of much relevance from a functional point of view.

It seems more useful to adopt the approach used in the *Grammar of Contemporary English* (Quirk *et al.*, Longman, 1972; Appendix 1) where an attempt is made to categorize prefixes by their meaning. There we have prefixes which are 'negative' (*un-*, *non-*, *in-*, *dis-*, *a-*), 'reversative or privative' (*un-*, *de-*, *dis-*), 'pejorative' (*mis-*, *mal-*, *pseudo-*), of 'degree or size' (*arch-*, *super-*, *out-*, *sur-*, *sub-*, *over-*, *under-*, *hyper-*, *ultra-*, *mini-*), 'attitude' (*co-*, *counter-*, *anti-*, *pro-*), 'locative' (*super-*, *sub-*, *inter-*, *trans-*), of 'time and order' (*fore-*, *pre-*, *post-*, *ex-*, *re-*), 'number' (*uni-/mono-*, *bi-/di-*, *tri-*, *multi-/poly-*); there are also 'conversion' prefixes (*be-*, *en-*, *a-*), and a miscellaneous category (*auto-*, *neo-*, *pan-*, *proto-*, *semi-*, *vice-*).

It is not difficult for any teacher equipped with a good dictionary to devise exercises which will familiarize his/her students with these prefixes. One such exercise is a straightforward matching exercise.

Example: Find the definition in the second column which matches the word in the first column.

Word		*Definition*
1	triple	A cycle with 3 wheels
2	trident	B stand or support with 3 legs
3	tripod	C series of 3 related books, plays, etc.
4	tricycle	D weapon with 3 points
5	trilogy	E grow (or cause to grow) to 3 times the original amount or number.

The technique of using prefixes to infer meaning can be practised.

Example: The prefix *mis-* is often used to give the sense of 'bad' or 'wrongly' or, occasionally, 'lack of'. See if you can work out the meaning of the words printed in *italics*.

(1)   There is a *misprint* in this newspaper.

(2)   I have *mislaid* my pipe.

(3)   He is an honest man, but his views are very *misguided*.

(4)   The politician complained that he had been *misquoted*.

(5)   You have *misunderstood* me.

(6)   He was accused of *misconduct* and dismissed from his job.

(7)   The workers viewed the new manager with some *mistrust*.

Suffixes can usually be related to a part of speech, indeed, they are often used to change one part of speech into another. So we have suffixes like *-ous* which are characteristically adjectival, and others like *-ify* which are characteristically verbal, and so on. Suffixes usually also have functional meanings. One of the best known of these is the *-er* suffix to denote an agent, i.e. the person or thing that does something: *teacher*, *writer*, *thriller* (kind of book), *receiver* (as in radio receiver), etc.

This can be the basis of a simple production exercise.

Example: The ending *-ify* is often used when something is caused or brought about by someone. For example, if a chemist turned something that was solid into a *liquid*, he might be said to have *liquified* it. Try to make up verbs in this way to give the meanings of the following sentences. You must form the verb from the word in *italics*. If you are in doubt, check up your dictionary first.

(1)   The research worker divided his material into different

      classes. He _____ his material.

(2)   The police are sure of the *identity* of the murderer. They

      have _____ him.

(3)   The ugly old witch filled the children with *terror*. She

      _____ them.

(4)   He put the book into *simpler* language. He _____

      the book.

(5)   He tried to show that what he had done was *just* and right.

      He tried to _____ what he had done.

Students should eventually be able to identify the more productive word-roots used in English, e.g. (from Latin: root–English equivalent–example word) *annus*–year–annual; *aqua*–water–aqueduct; *dens*–tooth–dental; *finis*–end–infinite; *verbum*–

word–verbal; *magnus*–great–magnify; *video*–see–vision; (from Greek) *metron*–measure–thermometer; *bios*–life–biology; *theos*–god–atheist, etc. It is *not*, however, recommended that this should be done by giving long lists of roots to remember, as this would probably be boring and confusing. Rather, words which are of similar derivation can be brought together and compared, e.g. *thermometer, barometer; gas-meter, parking-meter; kilometre, millimetre*. Looking at these examples, the student should not take too long to guess that *meter/metre* has something to do with 'measuring'. Whether the root-word is from Latin or Greek, or what its original form was, is probably of no particular interest or consequence to most learners.

Compounds

Sometimes new words are formed, not by adding a prefix or suffix to a base-word (as in anti-war [demonstration]), but by putting two or more base-words together, so that they form one unit as in *warhead* (the front part of a missile, containing explosives). Sometimes the compound is written as one word (*warhead*), sometimes with a hyphen (*war-cry*), sometimes as two words (*war memorial*). Sometimes words which have been joined together for a long time and are in frequent use (e.g. *headmaster*) are written together, whereas newer or less common compounds are hyphenated or printed as separate words. In general American English usage avoids the use of hyphenated forms. Usage is not always consistent in this area, and sometimes a reader will see the same compound written in all three ways.

Again as a general rule, stress in compounds is on the first syllable (compare *'greenhouse*, 'a glass building for growing plants under controlled conditions', with *'green 'house*, 'a house that has been painted green').

As far as teaching and learning the language are concerned, compounds do not give rise to many receptive problems. Compounds such as *headache, rainfall, theatre-goer*, etc. are fairly transparent. The main thing is that the learner should be alerted to the possibilities of inferring meaning by analysing the structure of such words. Occasionally compounds may be more opaque because they are compressed metaphors or they use association, e.g. *gate-crasher* 'someone who goes to a party that he/she has not been invited to', *egghead* 'intellectual', *hardhat* 'construction worker', *blue-collar/white-collar* 'manual/clerical' (workers) etc. Such forms are best learned as individual lexical items in context, and a short discussion of how they might have come to possess their current meaning might perhaps help to fix them in the learners' memory.

Productively, compound nouns can give rise to problems because they are not all formed in the same way. Some are noun + noun (*arrowhead*); some are verb + noun (*push-button*) and so on. Even compound nouns which are similar on the surface may have very different meanings, as we saw in Chapter 1, where *arrowhead* ('the head *of* an arrow') was contrasted with *armchair* ('a chair *with* arms') and other examples. There are literally hundreds of such variations, and there seems little point in any but the most advanced students of the language studying them systematically. What might be useful for intermediate to advanced learners is to look at some of the more productive *functional* types when examples offer themselves in context and to elicit other examples of the same functional type.

We may take, for example, *songwriter* ('someone who *writes songs*': note the singular form in the compound). This is a very productive type, and other examples can easily be elicited:

someone who reports on crime (*'crime reporter*)

.... pays taxes   (*'taxpayer*)

.... cleans windows (*'window-cleaner*)

.... plays tennis   (*'tennis-player*)

.... loves animals   (*'animal-lover*)

.... drives trucks   (*'truck-driver*)

.... teaches English (*'English teacher*, contrast with

English '*teacher*, 'a teacher
from England')

.... directs films   (*'film-director*: note spelling)

.... extracts teeth   (*dentist*! Foreign students have to
be careful not to invent 'original'
compounds.)

This exercise can also work in reverse, of course: compound nouns or phrases can be expanded in a fuller way. Some examples:

mud-covered wheels   → wheels that are covered in mud

well-trained soldiers   → soldiers who are well trained

a fast-moving train   → ....

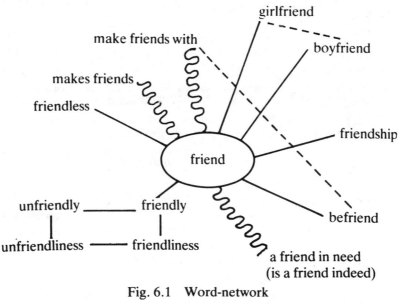

Fig. 6.1   Word-network

Word-networks

With more advanced students it is sometimes a useful idea to ask them to give you any words, phrases or proverbs that they know which are related to a common word (e.g. *friend*). Suggestions can be used to build up a 'word-network', as shown on Figure 6.1. Phrases and proverbs, etc. can be distinguished from other derived forms by using a wavy line, while words which have a special relationship (e.g. synonyms or antonyms) can be linked by a dotted line.

COLLOCATION

We have already seen that collocation, the way that words normally occur together, is something which permeates all language. The best way of picking up normal collocations is therefore by exposure to the target language in all sorts of different contexts. Some teachers would argue, however, that one of the reasons why learners have difficulty with producing the appropriate preposition in a given context is that such words are given very little emphasis in English speech: stress normally falls on 'content' words such as nouns or verbs. Some exercise books try to solve the 'preposition problem' by giving lists of sentences with blanks for where the prepositions should be. Such 'exercises' are, of course, really tests even when, as sometimes happens, a restricted range of possible prepositions is provided. It is, of course, possible to go on revising the sentences until the learner can pick the correct preposition every time, but this is boring and unmotivating.

A better idea would seem to be to focus attention on choice of appropriate preposition (or on any other aspect of collocation one is concerned with) *in an extended context*. When discussing a passage, the teacher should be careful to ensure that common collocations are made part of the question and answer process, although in most cases this will occur quite naturally anyway. Thus in the passage from *The Smuggler* given below, a question such as 'Where did Fame go?' might elicit the answer 'He *ran across* the street and *jumped into* his own car.' In answering the comprehension question, the student is also using the common verb + preposition collocation of *run across* and *jump into*.

A more elaborate technique is a combined listening and production exercise. The teacher prepares a passage in which certain words or expressions that he or she wishes to focus on have been deleted. An example might be the following passage. The teacher wishes to focus on prepositions and prepositional adverbs and has therefore *deleted* the words here printed in italics.

Fame ran *across* the street and jumped *into* his own car. He started the engine and accelerated *away* from the pavement. The American car was turning *into* the main road that went *out of* the town and *into* the hills. Fame followed it.

As long as they were in the town, Fame kept close *to* the American car. But when the two cars had left the town and were *on* the hill road, the more powerful American car moved further *ahead*. Fame could just read the car number, ZX 425. He wrote it *with* his finger *on* the dust *of* the window.

Then *in* another minute, Fame could no longer see the American car, but he kept going. He was driving *in* the hills *above* Dorna, looking *down over* the town and the lake. Fame knew the road well. He took it each time he came *to* Dorna. The road to Don's hideout turned *off* this road, a few miles *ahead*.

Well, Zara had told him to go and see Don, and at least he would get help there. Don was a member of their gang. Fame drove *on* as fast as he could. He was just coming *round* a long left hand bend when he saw a girl *in* a blue dress standing *at* the side of the road and waving *at* him. It was Zara. Fame put *on* the brakes and the car stopped.

'Get *in*!' he shouted.

(Piers Plowright, *The Smuggler*, Heinemann Guided Readers)

The teacher reads the whole passage aloud, *including the target prepositions*, giving the students time to fill in the blanks. The passage can then be read back to the teacher by individual students, or corrected as an exercise.

An alternative technique, without the listening phase, is to give the passage, with blanks as indicated, together with a list of the missing prepositions. Students check which prepositions go where; this can be done as a pair or group exercise. Occasionally more than one preposition is possible, and the teacher must be prepared for this. If students use vocabulary notebooks, they should be encouraged to record the normal collocations they come across as well as individual words: so as well as *good*, they may also have (*someone is*) *good at football/playing football*; (*something is*) *good for colds/curing colds* etc.

It is not only prepositional collocations that give rise to problems, of course. Other collocations (noun + noun, noun + verb, adjective + noun, verb + adverb, as well as more complex combinations) also have to be learned.

Let us take just one of these combinations as an example: noun + noun. A typical problem for the learner is selecting the appropriate word for the container in which things are stored. So we have a *box* of matches, but a *packet* of cigarettes. Typical containers, or units, in which things are bought may be elicited, or this may be the basis for a matching exercise. Some typical collocations are:

a *packet* of cigarettes	a *tin* (British)/*can* (American) of
cornflakes	beans
crisps	peas
salt	....
sugar	a *can/bottle* of beer
tea	a *bottle* of wine
....	....
a *pack* of (playing) cards	a *jar* of coffee
a *bag* of coal	marmalade

potatoes   ....

a *box* of   cigars   a *spool* of   thread

matches   a *ball* of   twine/rope

(also sometimes)

a *book* of   matches

a *length* of   cable/flex

and so on.

It must be emphasized again that the purpose of 'list' exercises like the above is basically to consolidate (and perhaps slightly expand) vocabulary already known. To use this technique as a method of expanding vocabulary on a large scale will probably just succeed in confusing the learner.

In an exercise in the previous chapter (p. 73: 'area of reference' exercise), we saw how words with roughly the same meaning can collocate differently, so we talk about a *partner* in a business, but an *accomplice* in crime, and an *ally* in war. That was, in fact, another example of typical noun + noun collocations. This can be done with other structural patterns, e.g. adjective + noun.

Example: Match the following adjectives with the nouns that they would usually go with:

Adjective		*Noun*	
1	calculated	A	retirement
2	deliberate	B	risk
3	voluntary	C	judgement
4	premeditated	D	mistake
5	considered	E	murder
6	express	F	ignorance
7	wilful	G	wish

For a quick classroom exercise, the letters could be matched to numbers, but it would probably be more beneficial to learners to write the phrases out. It is assumed that the learners are sufficiently advanced to understand the basic meanings of most or all of the vocabulary, even though they may not be familiar with the collocation itself.

Collocation exercises of this type need not necessarily use an advanced vocabulary. We can ask, for example:

How many ways can a person drive? (carefully, carelessly, dangerously, ...)
How many kinds of student are there? (bright, hard-working, lazy, dull, ...)
How many kinds of lesson are there? (exciting, dull, boring, difficult ...)

COHESION

In talking about compounds, we have been operating mostly at word level; in talking about collocations, mostly at phrase level; but when one discusses *cohesion* one is usually talking about higher units of language, typically the relationships between sentences or clauses. To clarify the discussion, let's look at these sentences:

'You'd better take an umbrella. The weather forecast is for rain.'

Although these are written as separate sentences, they clearly relate to one another in meaning: they are *coherent*. The coherence of the two sentences is mostly conveyed by the words/phrases *umbrella*, *weather forecast*, and *rain*, which are all related semantically. There are many phrases which could be associated with *an umbrella* which would still preserve the coherence of the two sentences: *a raincoat*, for example, or *your car*, but not (let's say) *a banana* or *a toadstool*.

The speaker could have gone further and made the logical relationship between the two sentences open or explicit: 'The forecast is for rain, so you'd better take an umbrella,' or 'You'd better take an umbrella, because the forecast is for rain.' We say that these sentences are not simply coherent, but also *cohesive* because the words *so* or *because* make the relationship explicit.

The reader may remember that we touched on this aspect of vocabulary before (p. 57), when we referred to such cohesive items as *so* and *because* using the terms *discourse markers* or *semantic markers*. (Many other terms exist: in the *Grammar of Contemporary English*, for example, they are called *logical connectors*.) We should think how such words and phrases can be identified in context and categorized according to the logical relationship they convey: cause-and-effect, opposition, etc.

Some teachers might wish to activate this aspect of vocabulary learning, by using productive exercises. A common technique used for this is to simply present some sentences from a text in jumbled order. Learners have to use discourse markers (and other cues) to rewrite the text in the normal way. This lends itself very well to small group activity; it is useful to have the sentences on separate slips of paper, so that they can be manipulated more easily.

Example: Rearrange the following sentences in the correct order.

(a) English and Dutch sailors made many attempts to discover it in the sixteenth century.
(b) The North-East passage is on the sea-way from the North Atlantic to the Bering Strait.
(c) Eventually, in the late nineteenth century, a Swedish explorer succeeded in finding it.
(d) These brave explorers were always defeated by ice.
     (Expected answer: badc)

After rearranging the sentences, the class can then discuss which features of the sentences enabled them to put the sentences in the correct order. These will probably include the pro-forms *these* and *it*, the time-connective *eventually*; and the fact that the phrases 'English and Dutch sailors' and 'these brave explorers' both refer to the same people (an example of what Halliday and Hasan [1976] have called 'lexical cohesion').

Alternatively, another well-established technique is the joining of simple sentences or phrases together, using connectors of various kinds, including pronouns (*he, they, the latter, this*, etc.). Some teachers build this in as a phase of composition writing. So, for example, the teacher may display a series of pictures showing a narrative (a road accident, someone losing a purse which is returned to her, and so on). Individual sentences are elicited which can then be made into a continuous narrative using the connectives previously written up on the blackboard.

VARIETY

There are many varieties of English: these may be different dialects (such as American English and British English) or different accents (such as General American, RP [Received Pronunciation], Irish and Scottish accents, etc.). But even within the standard dialects, there are many varieties according to:

the relationships between the speakers (formal or informal);
the nature of the subject or topic (law, science, the weather ...);
the context/situation in which the language occurs (a public meeting, a bar, one's home, an advertisement, a poem ...);
the function of the language (information, persuasion ...); and
the medium used (speech or writing).

Some linguists think of such variety within a standard dialect as being determined by the social situation, and like to speak of a certain *register* (e.g. 'legal register', 'scientific register', etc.). Other linguists think of such variety as basically being chosen by the speaker for his own purposes in a given situation and prefer to use the term *style*. (For a discussion of this, see O'Donnell and Todd, 1980.)

We can see that all this diversity of language makes it important to learn vocabulary in its natural context. This is the most effective way of tackling the problem of language variety. Sometimes we will wish to bring it to a learner's attention that a particular word is informal or very formal in its use, or that a certain expression is the appropriate one in dealing with a certain subject. An obvious example of this is the way in which we sign off letters. Apart from very informal letters (where anything is possible), there is a limited number of generally recognized ways of signing off: the two most common are *Yours faithfully* and *Yours sincerely*. So we have an example of language appropriate to a given situation. On top of this, however, there is a further formality distinction: *Yours faithfully* is more formal than *Yours sincerely*, and usually reserved for letters beginning *Dear Sir* or *Dear Madam*, rather than *Dear Dr Brown* or whatever, when *Yours sincerely* would be preferred.

One technique which is sometimes used to sensitize a foreign learner to how variety works in English is to put two different varieties of English side by side and ask the student to compare them. To make the contrast in language clearer, the varieties are sometimes on the same topic. In the following contrasting examples the topic is the same (announcement of rise in petrol prices), and they both are taken from newspapers, but one example is from *The Times* of London, a national 'up-market' newspaper, whereas the other example, is from the *Daily Record*, a popular provincial newspaper. Students might be asked to decide which excerpt came from which newspaper and identify the aspects of language which led them to make their choice:

It will be clear that the second extract is much more popular in its approach. What are the features of language which indicate this? It is, of course, not simply a matter of vocabulary: sentence and paragraph length come into it too, as well as other indicators such as the typography of the original reports. As far as vocabulary is concerned, students might be led to notice the choice of emotional words in the second excerpt: *fury, shock, shocked, enraged*; the use of highly charged words such as *massive, shooting-up, price-war zones, oil giant*; and (quoting) '*bleeding to death*'; and also the use of colloquial terms such as '*cash in on*'.

In the first excerpt, the language is more formal: we note *urban areas, spate of discounts, price support, dollar–sterling exchange rate*, and *imminent*.

Excerpt 1

Petrol going up 6-10p a gallon

by Edward Townsend

PETROL prices in Britain are set to rise by between 6p and 10p a gallon after the decision by BP Oil, the United Kingdom arm of British Petroleum, to withdraw its £1m-a-week price subsidy to garages from midnight tomorrow.

This increase means that motorists will be paying between 156p and 160p for a gallon of four-star. This could mark the end of the spate of discounts which has forced prices down in some urban areas to as low as 146p a gallon.

BP, whose action will also affect National filling stations, said it had been forced to end price support because of the sharp fall in the dollar–sterling exchange rate and the high cost of North Sea oil. In the first three months the company claimed to have lost £37m on its petrol and industrial fuel sales.

Some of the other big petrol suppliers, such as Shell, who are dependent largely upon North Sea oil, seem certain to follow the BP lead. Shell said yesterday a rise was imminent.

Excerpt 2

FURY AT THE PUMPS

(reported by
Malcolm McDougall)

FILLING up is to cost drivers up to 10p more for a gallon.

The shock new charges start at midnight tomorrow and stem from BP's withdrawal of their £1million subsidy to filling stations as a result of massive company losses.

And that will mean a gallon of four-star shooting up from an average of £1.50 to £1.56 or even £1.60 in Glasgow, Edinburgh, Aberdeen and other price-war zones.

Shocked motorists will be further enraged by the fact that other petrol companies, like Esso and Shell, look like following suit instead of cashing in on BP's higher prices.

A spokesman for one of the oil giants said: 'We are all bleeding to death.'

Similarly, in the general communicative area of 'invitation', students might study examples appropriate to different situations, perhaps with a view to using them as models for productive work.

Example 1

10th June

Dear Bill,

    I wonder if you and Joyce would like to come over and join us for dinner around 7 next Sunday? Sorry for the short notice — I've just heard that you're off to foreign parts again soon, and we'd like to see you before you go.

    Phone me if you can't make it.

Yours,
Jim

Example 2

                    7 Netherlea Drive
                    Edinburgh EH8 4AQ
                    (Tel: 031-338 6699)
                    10th June 1981

Dear Mr Jones,

    I wonder if you and your wife would be
free for dinner next Sunday evening (14 June)?
I must apologize for the short notice, but I've
only just heard that you're going abroad again
soon, and we'd like to have an opportunity of
saying goodbye to you before you go.

    If Sunday is not possible for you, please
let me know, and I'll see whether I can arrange
a more convenient time.

                    Yours sincerely,
                    James Brown

Invitations like these can be compared with each other and also
with formal invitation cards. Here again, vocabulary is part of a
larger context, in which layout, the kind of information given, etc,
are also important.

'Translation' from one variety of English into another (formal ↔
informal, technical ↔ plain language, and so on) is another possible
way of extending learners' productive skills in this area.

7 Vocabulary Games and Vocabulary Tests

It may seem strange to deal with the topics of vocabulary games and vocabulary tests in the same chapter, especially since they arouse such very different emotions in the learner! Yet when one comes to think of it, there is sometimes very little difference in *content* between games, tests, and exercises of the type that we have been discussing in the last two chapters. As we have already seen, it is very easy to convert many exercises into tests or games; and similarly tests can be transformed into games, games into tests, and so on.

Let us take as an example the 'Simple and Compound' game mentioned in George P. McCallum's *101 Word Games*, 1980. The *task* involved is for the reader to produce as many words as he or she can which contain the base-word *self* (e.g. *selfish*, *self-confident*, *myself*, *yourself*, etc.). This task may be tackled in three ways. First, as an *exercise*. The teacher's aim is to show how 'difficult' compound words may be formed from simple base-words which the student already knows. She asks the students to write down in their exercise books ten words containing *self*. She gives a few examples. While the students are working, she goes around correcting and advising. At the end of the lesson, the teacher gets some students to read their answers, and puts a selection of them on the blackboard.

Secondly, as a *game*. This teacher's aim is the same as the previous one, but he also wishes to add an element of fun or relaxation. He starts by dividing the class into four teams. After giving some examples, he tells the class that he is going to give them five minutes to write as many words as possible containing *self*. The words should be written on one sheet for each team. At the end of the five minutes the four team-leaders must come to the front of the class and read out what they have. There is one point for each word. Anyone may challenge a word and a dictionary will decide whether the word may be accepted. Points are added and one team declared the winner.

Thirdly, as a *test*. Here the teacher may have different aims: perhaps to check whether the students have done their homework; perhaps it is part of each student's continuous assessment to decide his/her place in class; and so on. The teacher gives a few examples, and then tells the students that they have three minutes to write down ten words containing *self*. They must work strictly on their own, and must not speak to their neighbours. The teacher monitors the class to make sure that no-one is cheating, and collects all the sheets at the end of the test to be marked and graded.

It will be seen that, although the students perform almost identical tasks in all three cases, there were important differences in the teacher's *aims* and in the *organization* of the task.

The basic aims of vocabulary games and vocabulary exercises are usually very similar: *to develop the student's vocabulary*, perhaps by extending his vocabulary or perhaps by giving him practice in using what he already knows receptively, and so on. In the vocabulary game there will be the additional aim (which may be more or less important according to circumstances) of adding an element of fun, relaxation and enjoyment to the lesson. Sometimes the fun element will be the main aim, and the teacher is not fussy about which area of language is being practised.

The purposes of tests, however, is usually *to supply information* on such matters as: how good is the student's command of vocabulary? What are his areas of weakness? How does his progress compare with that of other members of his class? And so on.

There are also obvious differences in organization. These will shortly be discussed when we look separately at vocabulary games and vocabulary tests. In the meantime, the reader might like to look back at the imaginary examples we gave, and to ask himself/herself what the differences were, and what the significance of these differences might be for his/her own teaching situation.

VOCABULARY GAMES

Language games have become more widely used recently, probably for two main reasons:

First, an increasing emphasis on the importance of motivation, and of the appropriate kind of positive affective atmosphere in the classroom.

Secondly, an increasing emphasis on the importance of 'real' communication. If a game is working properly, it very often supplies a genuine desire to communicate in the target language, even within the artificial confines of the classroom.

One of the characteristics of the organization of games is a competitive element. Hence the importance of scoring: it must be clear who has won, and the scoring system should be easy to work and obviously fair. The teacher often becomes a kind of 'referee': still an authority figure, but in a different way. The competitive element is often balanced by a co-operative element, especially when the class is divided into 'teams'. The members of each team co-operate for the success of their team.

Games usually have to be carefully organized, and clear, easily understood explanations must be prepared. Sometimes games have been designed for situations where classes are small and classroom furniture may be easily rearranged. Careful thought has to be given to these factors when using games in one's own situation.

Vocabulary is a teaching topic which lends itself very easily to the games approach, and there are literally hundreds of vocabulary games ranging from elementary to advanced level. All that will be attempted here is simply to give some examples relating to a few of the various areas which have already been discussed, namely *repetition*, *collocation* and *semantic field*. (Please note that only the central idea of the game is given: details of organization will have to be considered by the teacher for his/her own situation.)

REPETITION

The teaching purpose of these games is simply to bring to mind and revise vocabulary items which the student has already learned.

I spy
This is a very popular children's game. One of the players makes a mental note of something in the classroom (or on a wallchart, etc.), and the other players have to guess what it is. He gives them a clue by giving them the first letter of the target word. If the word were 'desk', for example, he would say: 'I spy with my little eye something beginning with ... D.'

Hidden object
Ten or twenty small objects are shown to the students, who name them. They are then put into a bag. The teacher picks up an object but *does not remove it from the bag*. A member of each team in turn is asked to guess what it might be. The first person to guess successfully is given the object. The team which ends up with most objects wins.

Jumbled letters
This can be also used to help with spelling difficulties. Teams are given letter-cards, each card containing one letter of the target

word thus: R E C E I V E . The letter-cards are

given out in random order, and the players have to rearrange them in the correct order. The first team to do this correctly wins.

What is it?
The teacher prepares some simplified drawings of everyday things, e.g. tables, chairs, houses, etc. He takes each object in turn and builds up the drawing of it on the blackboard, one line at a time. He pauses at the end of each line, and the players have to guess what he is drawing. The first player to guess correctly wins a point for his team.

Target picture
Each team is divided into so many pairs. One player in each pair has a photograph or a drawing of a scene. The other player has to attempt to draw the picture from his colleague's description, but

without seeing it: he must rely on the description alone. Dictionaries can be used. The teacher (whose decision is final!) awards 1, 2 and 3 points for the likeness. The team with most points wins.

COLLOCATION

Connections (Example from Wright, Betteridge and Buckby, 1979)
This has to be played quickly. Each player in turn says a word which he associates with the word given by the previous player. Sometimes the teacher or another player may ask the person who has just spoken to explain the connection he has made. For example:

> *Player 1*: Water.
> *Player 2*: Tap.
> *Player 3*: Shoulder.
> *Teacher*: Why did you say 'shoulder'?
> *Player 3*: Because I thought of the phrase, 'A tap on the shoulder!'

Key-word (Example from McCallum, 1980)
The class is divided into two teams and two students are chosen to represent each team (Team A and Team B). So there are four players: A1 and A2; B1 and B2. The players are at the front of the class, arranged like this:

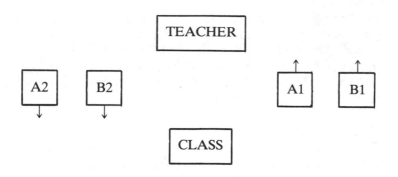

It will be seen that in each team one player is facing the teacher, and the other facing the class. The teacher holds up a card with a word printed on it. Let us say that the word is *shoe*. The players facing the teacher have to help their partners facing the class to guess the target word by calling out a word associated with the target word. So the game might go like this:

> Teacher holds up a *shoe*.
> *Player A1*: foot.
> *Player A2*: walk (wrong guess).
> *Player B1*: wear.
> *Player B2*: stocking (wrong guess).
> *Player A1*: leather.
> *Player A2*: shoe (wins the point).

Obviously, as the number of associations builds up it becomes easier to guess the target word.

Sally Smith (Example from McCallum, 1980)
A game for individual players. Each player has to say what Sally likes, but the answer must take the form of adjective + noun, both beginning with the letter S. The teacher points to players at random, who will say things like:

> Sally likes silk stockings.
> Sally likes silly stories.
> Sally likes scented soap.

And so on. For variation the name may be changed to Bob (letter B), Margaret (letter M), etc. The game should move quickly so it may be an idea to give the students a few minutes to prepare their answers.

SEMANTIC FIELD

Intruder
Either individual players or small teams. The teacher puts groups of

words in the same semantic field on the blackboard, but in each group there is one which does not belong, for example:

table, chair, cup, sofa, bed.

Cup is obviously the 'intruder', because it is not a piece of furniture. The players must spot the intruders and explain why they do not belong. At a more advanced level, teams could make up their own sets and challenge their opponents to spot the intruders.

Memory game
A team game. Players are shown a picture, slide, OHP or blackboard drawing containing a list of related items, e.g. animals, items of clothing or perhaps a scene. (If the students have picture dictionaries, then these can be used.) They are allowed to study the picture for a few minutes, after which it is removed. The members of each team pool their knowledge to see how many of the items they can remember. Items are written down as a check. The picture is shown again and the team with the highest score wins.

Furniture	
armchair	bed
bookcase	chair
cupboard	desk
fridge	sofa
stove	table
TV	wardrobe

Figure 7.1   Word Bingo Game

Word bingo (Materials package by Byrne, 1981)
The package consists of 'bingo boards' with lists of related words on them (see Figure 7.1). Each student is given a bingo board and a small number of 'cover-cards' which he uses to cover some of the words on the board, according to his choice. This means that the students will probably end up with different lists of words not yet covered. The teacher then calls out words at random from his copy of the bingo board. When a student hears a word that has not yet been covered on his board, he proceeds to cover it. The first student to cover all the words on his bingo board is the winner.

PENCIL-AND-PAPER GAMES

Another kind of fun activity which is very relevant to vocabulary study is the use of pencil-and-paper games such as crosswords and anagrams. Some publishers have produced crossword puzzle books which are graded according to difficulty (e.g. the *Crossword Puzzle Books* series by Hill and Popkin, OUP, is graded at elementary, intermediate and advanced levels). Once crosswords have been filled in, they cannot be used again, and to get round this problem Mary Glasgow Publications produce spirit duplicator masters of graded crosswords: from each master the teacher can duplicate up to 250 copies for class use. Another way of getting round the problem of filled-in crossword puzzles is to paste the crossword puzzles on cards and cover them with some sort of plastic bag or sheet. They can then be filled in by writing on the plastic sheet with a water-based pen; after use they can be wiped clean again.

Anagrams are easier for the teacher to make up, especially if they are simply jumbled letters (e.g. *napeelth* for *elephant*). More sophisticated anagrams (such as *they see* for *the eyes*) take much longer to devise! Anagrams may come in useful as a fun method for spelling revision. A variation of the anagram is the game of 'Wordfinder' where the players are given a word, and they have to see how many words they can make from the letters in it (e.g. *pencil* will give *lip*, *pen*, *nil*, *pile*, etc.). They are given a point for each acceptable word. Players should be allowed to use their dictionaries to check possible answers.

These examples we have looked at are only a small sample of the many hundreds of word-games and word-puzzles available. The point has already been made that the difference between an exercise and a game may be more a matter of organization than content. As with every other teaching technique, games and puzzles should be used with discretion, and especially with regard to the attitudes of the students involved. With some serious-minded students it may be advisable to make the games look more like exercises than vice versa!

VOCABULARY TESTS

A good teacher is always assessing his or her students' progress (or lack of it). In that sense, almost every question that the teacher asks is a kind of informal test. On occasion, however, the teacher will also feel the need to set a more formal type of test, and it is this type of test we are concerned with here.

It has been pointed out that the purpose of vocabulary tests is usually to·supply information; occasionally tests may have other purposes, of course, such as to motivate the students to study! If the purpose of a test is to supply information, then the information should be accurate.

Vocabulary tests should therefore be valid and reliable. A *valid* vocabulary test is one which tests what it is supposed to test. This may seem to be so obvious that it is hardly worth mentioning: yet it is surprising how many tests do not meet this basic requirement.

Let us take, for example, a test which is designed to find out whether students understand the meanings of certain words in a written context. The rubric (instructions) for the test may say: 'Give the meanings of the following words taken from the passage that you have just read': (then follows a list of words). What is wrong with this as a test of comprehension?

The problem is that it is possible to understand the meaning of a word without necessarily being able to *produce* another word (or phrase) which has the same meaning. This is therefore a test of *both* comprehension *and* production. If we are only interested in comprehension then we should adopt another testing strategy, perhaps by rewording the rubric thus: 'Look at the following list of word meanings. Opposite each one write down a word from the passage which has that meaning.' This involves the candidate only in matching the meaning with a word taken from the passage, a purely receptive skill.

A similar problem arises with the use of translation as a means of testing vocabulary. Let us imagine that a student has to translate a vocabulary item in a given context (it goes without saying that a student should never be tested by having to translate words out of context) from English to the mother tongue. If he or she gets it wrong, what have we been testing? Is it knowledge of the mother tongue: he knows what the word means but cannot find the exact way of expressing it? Or is it that his knowledge of English is faulty: he didn't understand the word in the first place?

This is not to say, of course, that translation is not a valid technique. It can be, of course: but the examiner must be clear about what it is exactly that he or she is testing.

Another example of tests which may not be valid often occurs with multiple-choice questions, which will be discussed later in this section. Sometimes the test-designer makes the multiple-choice question so difficult or tricky that what is being tested is not the understanding of the passage, but the understanding of the questions.

A *reliable* vocabulary test is one which will always give the same result under the same conditions. Fortunately, reliability is not usually such a great problem in vocabulary testing as it is in some other areas of language testing. In testing composition or testing conversational competence, for example, there is often a subjective element which has to be overcome, by using a detailed marking scheme, perhaps, and/or by using more than one examiner.

This is why the *multiple choice* technique, which we have just mentioned, is so popular as a testing device. Multiple-choice questions are usually organized so that the candidate has a number of *options*, only one of which is correct (the *answer*), the others (the *distractors*) being wrong. Here is an item taken from a language test on collocation (the candidate has to supply the missing word):

He has been accused _____ stealing the old lady's purse.

    A   with   C   in

    B   by   D   of

Only one of the options, D, is possible.

One of the main problems in making up multiple-choice tests is that the distractors have to be plausible (seem possible), with being misleading. This is what makes good multiple-choice questions difficult to write.

Example (Supply the missing word):

Is that gentleman married or _____?

    A   alone   C   bachelor

    B   single   D   without wife

All the options in the above question are in roughly the same area of meaning, but only B (*single*) sounds natural, since *married* and *single* are words which usually collocate as opposites. There is therefore a good chance of the distractors working. On the other hand, care must be taken not to unfairly mislead the candidate, as in the following example.

Example (Supply the missing word):

The sergeant showed the new _____ how to salute.

    A   volunteers   C   recruits

    B   conscripts   D   novices

The correct answer is given as C (*recruits*), but it could be argued that A (*volunteers*) and B (*conscripts*) are also possible.

Another testing procedure that is sometimes used for testing vocabulary is a *cloze test*. It should be said that cloze tests are claimed to be a general indicator of language proficiency, not only of vocabulary. Nevertheless various aspects of vocabulary competence certainly have a part to play in doing cloze tests, and they can be modified to emphasize this vocabulary aspect.

In a cloze test, a passage is taken and words are deleted from it at regular intervals (say, every fifth word, or every seventh word). The following passage has been taken from a simplified reader (Heinemann Guided Readers, Intermediate Level; rewritten by John Milne):

I think that was _____ happiest summer of my _____.

There was no trouble _____ our valley. Fletcher was _____

on business most of _____ summer. He was trying _____ get a

contract to _____ large amounts of beef _____ an Indian

Reservation some _____ away.

His men were _____ in the valley. But _____ kept to the other

_____ of the river and _____ not trouble us at _____. Some of

them were _____ friendly. It was Fletcher _____ made them do

things _____ troubled the homesteaders. Fletcher _____ us to

go away _____ used his men to _____ life difficult for us. _____

that Fletcher was away, _____ left us in peace.

(Jack Shaefer, *Shane*)

The reader might like to guess at the missing words and compare his or her answers with someone else's. What were the factors which led you to make your choice? Were they primarily matters of vocabulary, grammar, a mixture of the two, discourse, or something else again?

In comparing your own guesses with someone else's you may have come up with more than one word which seemed acceptable to you. Should the marking schedule accept everything that seems *acceptable* or only the *original word* used in the passage? The 'original word' method is more *reliable*, of course, but the other method seems more *valid* to many teachers.

Cloze tests may be modified in various ways. For example, the number of possible answers can be reduced, and the test made easier, by supplying the first letter of each word. So the first few sentences of our example would look like this:

I think that was t____ happiest summer of my l____.

There was no trouble i____ our valley. Fletcher was a ____ on a

business trip most of t____ summer. (etc.)

Other possibilities include: deleting only one class of word (nouns, verbs, prepositions, etc); deleting only certain chosen words; supplying a list of the missing words, so that they can be matched with the passage; and giving multiple-choice answers for each 'gap' or missing word. (These are gap-filling tests rather than real cloze tests).

We conclude this section by giving the original text for the cloze passage we have been using:

I think that was *the* happiest summer of my *life*.

There was no trouble *in* our valley. Fletcher was *away* on business most of *the* summer. He was trying *to* get a contract to *sell* large amounts of beef *to* an Indian Reservation some *distance* away.

His men were *still* in the valley. But *they* kept to the other *side* of the river and *did* not trouble us at *all*. Some of them were *even* friendly. It was Fletcher *who* made them do things *that* troubled the homesteaders. Fletcher *wanted* us to go away *and* used his men to *make* like difficult for us. *Now* that Fletcher was away, *they* left us in peace.

8 *Idioms and Multi-word Verbs*

In this final chapter we are going to look at two special areas of vocabulary which cause a lot of concern to EFL teachers and learners: idioms and multi-word verbs.

IDIOMS

Let us look at the area of *idioms* first. One of the problems is the problem of definition: the word *idiom* is often used in different ways to mean different things. Let us try, therefore, to establish a working definition.

Here are some idioms with their meanings:

let the cat out of the bag (= reveal a secret);
lick someone's boots (= humble oneself to gain someone's favour);
rain cats and dogs (= rain heavily);
storm in a teacup (= fuss about something that is not really important);
off the cuff (= not prepared beforehand).

(*Dictionary of English Idioms*, Collins, 1981)

What is it that they have in common? One could suggest two things. First, these expressions are *fixed collocations*. We have already seen that collocation is a feature of all language: this is what some people mean by language being 'idiomatic'. However, some collocations are fairly loosely related. When someone is trying to sell a house, for example, he or she might advertise it as a 'desirable residence'. Although this is a common collocation, it is not *fixed*.

One could, for example, use the words in all kinds of structures, such as 'a residence which many people would reckon to be desirable'; or the word *desirable* could be used with another word, as in 'desirable property for sale', and so on.

With idioms, this freedom of collocation is much more restricted. Using the examples we have noted, it would be odd to say:

they have let several cats out of bags (= revealed several secrets);
he goes about licking people's sandals;
yesterday it rained dogs and cats;
the teacup has just had a storm;
he made an off-his-cuff remark,
and so on.

It is true that certain changes are possible. For example, *rain cats and dogs* can be used in any tense, past, present or future. In the expression *lick someone's boots*, there is really a gap in the middle of the expression which can be filled with any name, title, etc. Generally speaking, however, idioms operate in some ways as if they were compound words, and the number of changes that can be made are very limited.

The second important thing which all idioms have in common is that they cannot be decoded (understood) from the literal or ordinary meaning of the words they contain: we can say that they are *semantically opaque*. Going back to our examples, we can take *let the cat out of the bag* or *rain cats and dogs*. The meanings of these expressions have no obvious connections with cats, dogs or bags! Some idioms are less opaque (or, to put it another way, more transparent) than others. For a foreign learner, it might be easier to guess the meaning of *lick someone's boots* than *let the cat out of the bag*: but this might also depend on the amount of help the learner got from the context. However, if the meaning of a fixed collocation is perfectly obvious from the words which make it up, then we would say it is 'transparent' and therefore not an idiom. An example would be the expression *Pleased to meet you* often used by people who are being introduced. The meaning of this fixed collocation is easily understood from the words which make it up, and it is therefore not an idiom.

There is one assumption we have been making (which many linguists would not make) and it is that an idiom consists of *more than one word*. Makkai (1972) argues, for example, that a compound like *blackmail* is an idiom because its meaning cannot be decoded from *black + mail*; Chafe (1970) states that any word not used in its literal sense is an idiom.

These examples show that there is no generally accepted linguistic definition of 'idiom' (any more than there is, one might say, of most other basic language terms!). However, it could be suggested that a practical definition of 'idiom' for teaching purposes will contain three elements:

(1)   idioms consist of more than one word;
(2)   idioms are fixed collocations; and
(3)   idioms are semantically opaque.

TEACHING IDIOMS

What are the teaching implications of these points which we have been making concerning idioms?

First of all, there does not seem to be any point in grouping idioms together, and teaching them together, simply because of some words they have in common. In some books for teaching idioms, for example, several idioms which happen to mention animals (e.g. *let the cat out of the bag*; *rain cats and dogs*; *lead a dog's life*, etc.) are taught together. This is pointless since, as we have just seen, the literal meaning of the words has little or nothing to do with the real meaning of the idiom. It is a bit like teaching the words *football* and *ballroom* together, because they both contain the word *ball*!

The most sensible thing, in fact, is to treat idioms as unusually long words, and to teach them as one would any new word: that is, as they occur in a meaningful context. It may be useful to indicate what changes the idiom can undergo, and this often relates to the idiom's underlying meaning (see Chafe, 1970). Let us return to an example we have used often, *let the cat out of the bag*. It is possible to make this expression passive and say: *the cat's been let out of the bag*. This is possible because the underlying meaning ('reveal a secret') can also be made passive ('the secret has been revealed'). An expression like, *it was raining cats and dogs* ('it was raining heavily') obviously cannot be made passive because of the underlying meaning. But this will not always explain what is possible and what is not possible as far as altering the structure of idioms is concerned, and learners may need some help on this.

It is important that idioms should not be confused with colloquial language or slang. Colloquial language is used when people are speaking informally and it may contain idioms, but not necessarily. Slang means informal words or expressions used by a particular group of people (e.g. young people), usually to distinguish themselves from others. Again, slang often contains idioms, but not necessarily. So idioms are not something 'special' or 'sub-standard': they are a vital part of the standard language, and as such can hardly be avoided.

To sum up, then, we can say that idioms are a special form of collocation which will be encountered by every learner. Although there have been various attempts to classify idioms, there seems little to be gained by dealing with idioms under different linguistic categories. They are best treated as individual lexical items, to be learnt as such.

MULTI-WORD VERBS

A multi-word verb is a verb plus a particle (i.e. preposition or adverb), or, sometimes, a verb plus two particles, which join to form a new structural unit. Here are some examples of multi-word verbs:

abide by	cave in	mow down	take in
add up	cross off	own up	take on
become of	do without	parcel up	while away
burn down	give up	puff away	work out
come down with		cut back on	
get off with		stand up to	

The vast majority of multi-word verbs contain the following particles (most common particles listed first): *up*, *out*, *off*, *down*, *in*, *away*, *on*, *back*, *about*, *over*, *around*, *through*.

It is simpler to discuss multi-word verbs if we first of all recognize that there are two main kinds of multi-word verbs. These are usually called *phrasal verbs* and *prepositional verbs*, and this is the way that they will be referred to in this chapter. Some writers, however, find it useful to call them *separable verbs* and *fused verbs*, for reasons that will shortly become clear.

TEACHING MULTI-WORD VERBS

There are three main areas of error with respect to multi-word verbs:

(1)   in productive language, the use of the wrong particle with the verb – a problem of collocation;
(2)   receptively, not being able to understand these multi-word verbs which are also idioms;
(3)   generally, problems arising from the special nature of these verbs: their different structural patterns (e.g. with pronouns), their special stress patterns, and so on.

PREPOSITIONAL VERBS

Look at these two sentences. Which one contains the prepositional verb?

(1)   She always looked after her father when he was ill.
(2)   Jane arrived after her uncle, who was early.

It is, of course, the first sentence which contains the prepositional verb (*looked after*), whereas the second sentence contains the verb plus preposition, *arrived* + *after*. Because it is a structural unit, transformations can be applied to *looked after* which cannot be applied to *arrived* + *after*. *Look after* can, for example, be made passive: he was always looked after by his daughter when he was ill.

The second sentence cannot be made passive.

Look after, like many other prepositional verbs, is not only a structural unit, it is also a *semantic unit.* By this we mean that the verb and the particle have lost some or all of their original sense to form a new unit of meaning – in other words, it is an 'idiom', as we defined it earlier in this chapter.

The fact that prepositional verbs are structural units, and in most cases also semantic units, has implications for the way they should be taught. It means that there is little point in grouping prepositional verbs by either the verb or the particle. In some textbooks, prepositional verbs are presented in lists in this way, e.g. *look after, look for, look to, look over* (= survey), *look through* (= inspect) might be presented at the same time. This is simply confusing for the learner.

Prepositional verbs should be taught as individual lexical items as they arise in context. Students should learn prepositional verbs as a unit, so that they realize that the particle is an integral part of the verb it goes with.

PHRASAL VERBS

Like prepositional verbs, phrasal verbs are structural units. The main difference in this respect is that with phrasal verbs the verb is often separated from its particle. So we can say:

Put down that book! or
Put that book *down*!

Indeed the second sentence is perhaps the normal ('unmarked') form of a phrasal verb and its object. Of course a prepositional verb cannot be separated in this way.

The difference is even more striking if the object noun phrase is a pronoun, such as *him, her, it,* etc. In that case the pronoun nearly always comes between the verb and its particle:

Put it down!
Look it up! (= check it in a reference book, etc.)
Take it away!

Very occasionally, if attention is being focused on the pronoun (perhaps for emphasis or contrast), then it may come after the particle in a phrasal verb:

I told you to call him up (= telephone him), but
I told you to call up *him*, not her.

In normal speech particles are not usually given stress, but with phrasal verbs the particle normally receives stress. Compare:

'Call 'up that number – that's the number to 'call 'up.
with:

'Look for that number – that's the number to 'look for.

One way into the typical patterning of phrasal verbs is by starting with the most literal or 'transparent' examples, which can be easily situationalized in the classroom:

Put your books *down*.
Take these books *back* to the library.
Write these words *down*.

Such examples transform easily into: Put them down/Take them back/Write them down. A transformation drill along these lines may be useful sometimes, especially from the point of view of familiarizing learners with typical stress patterns.

In their reading, students may come across examples where the object noun phrase is shifted to after the particle. This usually happens when the object noun phrase is a long one, or sometimes for emphasis, or sometimes simply for reasons of style.

After looking at some examples, an exercise could be done in the following way.

Example. In the following sentences, the phrases in *italics* have all been put after the particle. Say which ones could be naturally placed before the particle, in the position marked X.

(1)   Take X down *these notes.*
(2)   Take X back *the book you borrowed from the library.*
(3)   I told you to pick X up *your pencils, not your pens.*
(4)   He's smashed X up *his new car.*
(5)   I hope you've packed X away *enough clothes to keep you warm.*

If a teacher decides to cover the meaning aspect of phrasal verbs systematically, and it might be argued that this ought to be done at some stage in most comprehensive courses, the best strategy is probably to concentrate on the *particle.* (For a very good working-out of this approach, see McArthur, 1973.)

We have seen that the meaning of the phrasal verb (and, therefore, of the particle) can often be quite easily understood, e.g.: *lift up, raise up, take down,* etc. On many occasions the particle is understandable in an extended sense: for example, *burn down* (a house), *keep down* (prices), *wipe off* (a stain), etc. These extended senses can usually be guessed by learners if presented in context.

One of the features which is often overlooked in teaching phrasal verbs is that the particles of such verbs often develop special meanings. The particle *up,* for example, is used with many verbs to give a sense of 'completeness' as in these examples: *fill up, finish up, load up, open up, tear up. Down* is often used in a similar way, but sometimes with a negative sense: *close down, cut down, melt down. Away* can be used to give the meaning of continuous action: *hammer away, work away, write away.*

Once examples of these meanings have been met with in context, students can be asked to give other examples from their vocabulary store, or to guess the meanings of sentences provided by the teacher.

(*away = continuous action*)

They used to argue away all evening.
He furiously banged away with his hammer.
We found them merrily eating and drinking away.
I came an hour later, and there she was, still talking away.

There are many phrasal verbs, of course, which are complete idioms and have to be learnt as units, e.g. *show someone up* (= humiliate), *make something up* (= invent), *smoke someone out* (= expose) and so on.

There are other teaching points in the area of multi-word verbs for which exercises can be devised. We could deal with derived noun-forms, for example, by devising a simple transformation exercise (examples would have to be analysed first, of course):

	Cue	*Answer*
1	She has started making up her face.	
	She has started to use _____.	(make-up)
2	The supply of food has broken down. There	
	has been a _____ in the food supply.	(breakdown)
3	They have mixed up the exam papers. There's	
	been a _____ with the exam papers.	(mix-up)
4	Our plane took off very smoothly.	
	We had a very smooth _____.	(take-off).

Idioms and multi-word verbs present many similarities in treatment from a teaching and learning point of view, largely because they occupy overlapping areas in language. Multi-word verbs are more capable of systematic treatment in certain respects, as we have indicated. As in other areas of vocabulary, most of the learning should be done in a realistic language context, if possible; exercises and drills should be confined to those occasions where such systematic treatment can speed the learner on towards his goal of mastery of the target language.

Suggestions for Further Reading and Discussion/Activity

CHAPTER 1

Further reading
The references in this chapter are:

J. A. Bright, 'The training of teachers of English as a second language in Africa', in G. E. Perren, *Teachers of English as a Second Language: Their Training and Preparation* (CUP, 1968).

H. Kucera and W. N. Francis, *Computational Analysis of Present Day American English* (Brown University Press, 1967).

G. Leech, *Semantics* (Penguin Books, 1974). (2nd ed., 1982).

A. Lehrer, *Semantic Fields and Lexical Structure* (North Holland, 1974).

C. K. Ogden, *The General Basic English Dictionary* (Evans, 1940).

M. West, *A General Service List of English Words* (Longman, 1953).

A useful, up-to-date word-list is:

R. Hindmarsh, *Cambridge English Lexicon* (CUP, 1980). It is based on various word-counts including GSL and the Brown Corpus.

On the subject of academic vocabulary, see:

J. Praninskas, *American University Word List* (Longman, 1972).

The dictionaries referred to are:

Collins Dictionary of the English Language (Collins, 1979). (Abbreviated in text to CED).
Longman Dictionary of Contemporary English (Longman, 1978).

Further reading on semantics might include the books by Leech and Lehrer just referred to, which are both, however, fairly technical in parts. A general book on linguistics which covers this topic in a very clear and interesting way is D. Bolinger, *Aspects of Language*, 3rd ed. (Harcourt Brace Jovanovich, 1981). Another useful introduction is F. R. Palmer, *Semantics – A New Outline*, 2nd ed. (CUP, 1981).

Suggestions for discussion/activity
(1)   Vocabulary and grammar. In what situations would a non-native speaker of a language still be able to communicate if he knew only some vocabulary (i.e. isolated words) and had no knowledge of the grammar (system) of the target language? In what circumstances, and how, might he be able to communicate if he had no knowledge of the language *at all*? As a language teacher, what conclusions would you draw from this?
(2)   Word frequency.   (a)   Look at the following passage. The word *thousand* is not listed in the General Service List (GSL), since it does not contain days, months or numbers. The passage also contains *eight* other words which are not listed in the GSL as being among the 2000 most common words in English. Can you guess which ones? (Answers at the end of this section.)

My father was a fine mechanic. People who lived miles away used to bring their cars to him for repair rather than take them to the nearest garage. He loved engines. 'A petrol engine is sheer magic,' he said to me once. 'Just imagine being able to take a thousand different bits of metal ... and if you fit them all together in a certain way ... and then if you feed them a little oil and petrol ... and if you press a little switch ... suddenly those bits of metal will all come to life ... and they will purr and hum and roar ...

they will make the wheels of a motor-car go whizzing round at fantastic speeds ...'

> (Roald Dahl, *Danny, the Champion of the World*
> [Heinemann Educational Books 1975].)

(b)   What is the usefulness of a word frequency list to a teacher?

(3)   Availability. What words are 'available' in the classroom? How would you rate them for usefulness outside the classroom?

(4)   Learnability. Look again at the passage quoted in 2(a). Which of the less common words in that passage would be most easily learned/taught? Which would be difficult to learn/teach? What would you say are the factors in making a word more easily or less easily learned?

(5)   Denotation.   (a)   List some of the possible denotations of the following words:

foot; late; fresh; dead; small; switch.

What is the basic meaning or denotation of each of these words? Which of the other denotations would you say were easily 'guessable', and which difficult to guess, if one knew the basic meaning?

(b)   If you know another language apart from English (or if you have a good bilingual dictionary), choose an English word and its most common equivalent in the other language. Compare and contrast the range of denotations of the two words.

(6)   Association. Can you think of any words (like *market*) which might have different associations in different countries?

Note: In exercise 2(a), the eight words in the passage which are not listed in the GSL are:

1 petrol   2 sheer   3 magic   4 switch   5 purr   6 hum
7 whizzing   8 fantastic.

CHAPTER 2

Further reading
The reference in this chapter is:

A. Burgess, *A Clockwork Orange* (Penguin Books, 1972).

The passage used in Exercise 2 below is from:

J. Schaefer, *Shane*, Heinemann Educational Books, Guided Readers series, 1973. Rewritten by J. Milne.

There are useful discussions on the teaching of vocabulary in:

J. A. Bright and G. P. McGregor, *Teaching English as a Second Language* (Longman, 1970).
W. M. Rivers and M. S. Temperley, *A Practical Guide to the Teaching of English as a Second or Foreign Language* (New York: OUP, 1978).

Graded readers. The reader will find useful information on graded readers in a companion volume to this one by C. Nuttall, *Teaching Reading Skills in a Foreign Language*, Practical Language Teaching Series no. 9 (Heinemann Educational Books, 1982).
    A brief but very useful guide to readers has been published by the British Council. It is C. J. Brumfit, *Readers for Foreign Learners of English* (The British Council, 1979). This contains a comprehensive list of titles graded by difficulty, a list of publishers' addresses, and a bibliography on grading.

Graded magazines. Again, the British Council provides a very useful service to language teachers by issuing a regularly updated leaflet called *Simplified Language Magazines* (Specialised Bibliography B11), Central Information Service, The British Council. The leaflet covers magazines for students of English as a Foreign Language, French, German and Spanish. The various EFL magazines are:

(1)   Berry Newsmagazines, Darby House, Merstham, Redhill RH1 3DN, England:
    You (beginners level); *People* (2nd year students); *Faces and Places* (3rd year students); *News and Views* (4th year

students); *Inside Britain and America* (advanced).

(2) Chatterbox Publications, 3 College Road, Thurlton, Norwich, NR14 6OZ, England:
Junior Chatterbox (elementary); *Senior Chatterbox* (intermediate).

(3) De Sikkel, Nijverheidsstraat 3, 2150 Malle, Belgium:
English Pages: Start (advanced).

(4) Eilers and Schünemann, Postfach 919, Bremen 1, FRG (UK Distributor: Bookpostgiro, 39 Church Road, Watford WD1 3PY, England):
International World and Press (extracts from English and American publications with vocabulary for students).

(5) Linguapress (11 Place Victor Hugo), 25000 Besançon, France:
Horizon (adults, beginners); *Freeway* (adults, intermediate); *Spectrum* (adults, advanced).

(6) Mary Glasgow Publications, Brockhampton Lane, Kineton, Warwicks, England:
Click (absolute beginners, 9–12 years old); *Crown* (elementary, 10–13 years old); *Clockwork* (2nd or 3rd year, 11–14 years old); *Catch* (intermediate, 13–15 years old); *Club* (intermediate, 15–17 years old); *Current* (advanced students).

(7) Modern English Publications, 8 Hainton Avenue, Grimsby, South Humberside, DN32 9BB, England:
Business Express (with cassette; for self-study work in English for business).

(8) Editions Fernand Nathan (UK Distributor: Modern English Publications – see above):
Speakeasy, Easy Speaking.

(9) J. Van In, Belgium (UK Distributor: Modern English Pubications – see above):
Pace (Advanced).

(10) Wolters-Noordhoff-Longman, Afdeling Periodeken, Postbus 58, Groningen, The Netherlands:
Quads (articles from four British newspapers).

Suggestions for discussion/activity

(1) How far do you think that the principles of learning vocabulary in the mother tongue should also apply to learning vocabulary in a foreign language?

(2) (a) Read the passage which follows. Examine the words underlined, and rate them in terms of how 'guessable' they are in this context. (Assume that the students know all the words in the passage except those underlined.) Use this scale to rate the words, putting the numbers 1–5 in the spaces provided at the end of the passage.

Impossible to guess		*Reasonably 'guessable'*		*Very easy to guess*
1	2	3	4	5

The *mysterious* stranger appeared one summer afternoon in 1899. I was only ten years old at the time and I was enjoying my long summer holiday. Most of the time I did nothing and enjoyed myself sitting in the sun.

That summer afternoon I was sitting in the sunshine on the upper rail of our small *corral* when I saw the stranger coming on horseback towards our house.

In the clear air, I could see him plainly although he was still several miles away. There seemed at first nothing unusual about him. He seemed just like another stranger riding up the road towards our town. Then I saw two *cowboys* going past him. They stopped and stared after him very carefully.

As he came nearer, I noticed his clothes. He wore dark-coloured trousers and tall *leather* boots. He also wore a broad leather belt. His shirt was dark brown and his coat, made of the same material as his trousers, was thrown over his *saddle* in front of him.

He had a handkerchief of black silk *knotted* round his throat and his hat was unusual. It was made of a soft black material that I had never seen before. His hat had a wide *brim* which came down in front of his face.

He had no beard or *moustache*. His face was *lean* and hard and it was burned with the sun. His eyes seemed covered by the broad brim of his hat. But as he came nearer, I could see that they were *alert* and looking for any danger. I could see that he was noticing everything that he passed. And he rode easily on his horse like a man who has lived in the saddle.

(Jack Shaefer, Shane)

The underlined words were:

mysterious _____; corral _____; cowboys _____;
leather _____; saddle _____; knotted _____;
brim _____; moustache _____; lean _____; alert _____.

(b)   Justify your decision: why did you think the words were easy/difficult to guess? (Do not, at this stage, worry about how you would *teach* these words. We shall be coming back to this in the next chapter.)

(3)   On p. 34 it says 'a *class* library is perferable to a *school* library, as far as English readers are concerned'. Do you agree? How would you organize a class library *or* a school library to improve foreign language reading skills?

CHAPTER 3

Note: I am grateful to my colleague Patricia Ahrens for allowing me to base the transcript used at the beginning of this chapter on a microlesson which she taught.

Further reading
The references in this chapter are:

Science Research Associates, *SRA Reading Laboratory Level II B* (Science Research Associates, Henley-on-Thames, Oxfordshire RG9 1EW, 1965).
F. Smith, *Understanding Reading* (Holt Rinehart, 1971).

Suggestions for discussion/activity

(1)   Go back to the passage from *Shane*. Take one or more of the words you have judged to be 'guessable' and show/discuss how you would elicit the meaning of the word(s) from a learner.

(2)   Choose an everyday function of language (e.g. asking the time from a stranger/buying an airline ticket, etc.). Make a list of the vocabulary which is particular to that function in a particular situation. Compare your list with others. Show/discuss how you would present and practise that vocabulary situationally with a class.

(3)   (a)   What would you say is the most effective way of presenting new vocabulary?

(b)   What are the advantages and disadvantages of elicitation as a technique for teaching vocabulary?

CHAPTER 4

Further reading
The references in this chapter are:

P. Meara, 'Vocabulary acquisition: a neglected aspect of language learning, Survey Article, *Language Teaching and Linguistics Abstracts:* vol. 13, no. 4 (Oct. 1981), pp. 221–46.

P. Nation, 'Strategies for receptive vocabulary learning', in *Guidelines for Vocabulary Teaching* (Regional English Language Centre, Singapore, 1980).

L. Sandosham, 'Using the word bank as a vocabulary building aid', also in *Guidelines for Vocabulary Teaching.*

M. J. Wallace, *Study Skills in English* (CUP, 1980).

Suggestions for discussion/activity

(1)   *Read again the passing from Shane* on p. 130. What 'semantic clusters' (i.e. groups of words related by meaning in some way) can you find? Can they be exploited for teaching purposes?

(2)   Look at any textbook that has comprehension passages. How is the vocabulary teaching handled? Could it have been done in a different way?

(3) Choose ten words in any language you know and write down their equivalents in English. Choose words which are very different in form from English. Try to make 'meaning bridges' between the English words and their translations. Compare your 'bridges' with your friends'. How useful do you think this technique might be for a foreign language learner?

CHAPTER 5

Further reading
The references in this chapter are:

C. Alderson and G. Alvarez, 'The development of strategies for the assignment of semantic information to unknown lexemes in text', *Mextesol Journal*, vol. 2, no. 4, pp. 46–55.
D. L. F. Nilsen and A. P. Nilsen, *Semantic Theory – A Linguistic Perspective* (Newbury House, 1975).
F. Forsyth, *The Devil's Alternative* (Corgi, 1979).

There are now many EFL dictionaries on the market for learners at all levels. Two very useful titles for advanced learners are:

Longman Dictionary of Contemporary English (Longman, 1978).
Oxford Advanced Learners Dictionary of Current English, 3rd ed. rev. (OUP, 1980).

Teachers' guides and/or students' workbooks for these dictionaries are also available.
A typical example of a useful elementary 'picture dictionary' is:

E. C. Parnwell, *Oxford English Picture Dictionary* (OUP, 1977).

On the same lines, but done much more fully and elaborately for advanced learners is:

The Oxford-Duden Pictorial English Dictionary (OUP, 1981).

Another useful reference work for the EFL teacher is *Roget's Thesaurus*, which groups together words and phrases which have a similar meaning. In other words, words and phrases are arranged according to the idea they express rather than by alphabetical order, as in a normal dictionary. A thesaurus is therefore a good source for synonyms and antonyms. Many different editions exist, for example:

Roget's International Thesaurus, 4th ed. (Harper & Row, 1979).
Roget's Thesaurus (Longman, 1981).

The problem with the normal thesaurus is that it is intended for native speakers, so the related words are simply listed and not defined. A very useful reference work which does not have this drawback, and has been written especially with foreign learners in mind, is:

T. McArthur, *Lexicon of Contemporary English* (Longman, 1981).

This book is a combined thesaurus, dictionary and picture dictionary of some 15,000 items.

Suggestions for discussion/activity
(1)   Take a passage from a book and blank out some of the words, perhaps about 1 in 10. Show it to a colleague and see if you can lead him to guess the missing words, without directly telling him what they are. What techniques did you use, and how effective were they? (It will be easier to answer or discuss the last questions, if you can audiotape your elicitation of the missing words.)
(2)   The following pairs of lexical items might be called 'synonyms':

Journey/voyage; arrive at/reach; modest/humble; looking glass/ mirror; error/mistake; proud/arrogant; habit/custom; pair of/ two; like/enjoy; grow/increase.

(a)   In what contexts might these words be substituted for each other, and in what contexts might they *not*? (Sometimes the decisions may be difficult to make. A good dictionary might be helpful.)

(b)   Is it useful to make distinctions between such words with learners? If it is, how would you go about doing so?

(3)   It is said that *borrow/lend* and *husband/wife* have 'reciprocal meanings'. Can you think of any other words which also have a reciprocal meaning relationship? Which of them might give rise to learning problems?

CHAPTER 6

Further reading
The references in this chapter are:

W. R. O'Donnell and L. Todd, *Variety in Contemporary English* (Allen & Unwin, 1980).

R. Quirk, S. Greenbaum, G. Leech and J. Svartvik, *A Grammar of Contemporary English* (Longman, 1972).

P. Plowright, *The Smuggler,* Guided Readers Series (Heinemann Educational Books, 1974).

A very comprehensive account of cohesion is:

M. A. K. Halliday and R. Hasan, *Cohesion in English* (Longman, 1976).

Suggestions for discussion/activity
(1)   Look at the list of prefixes on p. 86. See how many of them you can get examples for which illustrate the meaning that is given.

(2)   On p. 88 are listed some of the more productive word-roots in English. Are there any more roots that you would like to add to that list? (You can quote the roots in the form[s] in which they occur in English, not in the original language. If you are stuck for ideas, glancing through a dictionary might help you.)

(3)   Look again at Figure 6.1. Try to make up 'word networks' for these words (or, better still, some words of your own choice):

poor; public; school; sense; simple; think.

(4)   Pick a set of words (some suggestions below). Go round your colleagues, or ask your students, if they are sufficiently advanced, what word or short phrase would go with the word. For example, with *run* one person might say 'run a race', another 'run a mile', and so on. Find out which are the most popular collocations for each word. Suggestions: run _____; in _____; set _____; first _____; just _____.

CHAPTER 7

Further reading
The references in this chapter are:

English Crosswords: 3 sets of Spirit Duplicator Masters (Set 1 – 1st/2nd year level; Set 2 – 2nd/3rd year level; Set 3 – 3rd/4th year level) (Mary Glasgow Publications).
D. Byrne, *Word Bingo* (Modern English Publications, 1981).
L. A. Hill and P. R. Popkin, *Crossword Puzzle Books* (Books 1–4: Elementary–Advanced) (OUP).
G. P. McCallum, *101 Word Games* (New York, OUP, 1980).
A. Wright, D. Betteridge and M. Buckby, *Games for Language Learning* (CUP, 1979).

Other material may be found in, for example:

C. Granger and J. Plumb, *Play Games with English* (Books 1 and 2) (Heinemann Educational Books, 1980, 1981).
W. R. Lee, *Language-Teaching Games and Contests* (OUP, 1965).
R. Ridout, *Puzzle it Out* (Books 1–5) (Evans).

On testing, a useful introduction, which contains a section on testing vocabulary, is:

J. B. Heaton, *Writing English Language Tests* (Longman, 1975).

Suggestions for discussion/activity
(1)   How important would you say games are in language-teaching methodology? Are they just a source of fun for Friday afternoon or the end of term, or do they have a more important role to play?

(2)   Pick a language game which you might want to use in your own language-teaching situation. (It could be one of those described, or one of your own). Explain very precisely and clearly:

(a)   how you would organize the class;
(b)   what instructions etc. you would give the players before the game began.

(3)   What are the reasons that a teacher might wish to use a formal vocabulary test (see p. 111 above)?

(4)   (a)   Look through the exercises listed in Chapters 5 and 6. Which of them could be made into:

(i)   games, and/or
(ii)   tests?

(b)   Would they have to be modified in any way to make them into useful games/tests?

CHAPTER 8

Further reading
The references in this chapter are:

W. Chafe, *Meaning and the Structure of Language* (University of Chicago Press, 1970).
A. Makkai, *Idiom Structure in English* (The Hague, Mouton, 1972).
T. McArthur, *Using Phrasal Verbs* (Collins, 1973).
M. J. Wallace, *Dictionary of English Idioms* (Collins, 1981).

The standard reference work on idioms in English is:

A. P. Cowie and R. Mackin, *Oxford Dictionary of Current Idiomatic English* (OUP, Vol. 1, 1975; Vol. 2, forthcoming).

A very clear introduction to the subject of multi-word verbs is to be found in the *Grammar of Contemporary English* by Quirk and others, already referred to several times.

Suggestions for discussion/activity
(1)   (a)   Try to arrange the following fixed collocations in order, according to how transparent/opaque they are. Which of them would you say were idioms according to the way the word has been defined in this chapter? (Leave room for disagreement!)

   (i)   to count one's chickens before they're hatched
  (ii)   to have a chip on one's shoulder
 (iii)   to be half-hearted (about doing something)
  (iv)   to make up one's mind
   (v)   to see red
  (vi)   what rotten luck!
 (vii)   to sleep round the clock
(viii)   good riddance to bad rubbish!
  (ix)   as a rule (something happens)
   (x)   to run short of (food etc.)

   (b)   Can you make up short contexts which would make their meanings clear to learners?
   (2)   (a)   In the chart on p. 139 are some common verbs and particles. Put an X to show where they can combine to form multi-word verbs. The multi-word verbs *get out*, *carry off*, and *put up* are done as examples.
   (b)   Which of the resulting verbs are phrasal and which prepositional? In this sample, which particles seem to form mostly phrasal verbs, and which mostly prepositional verbs?

	above	away	by	down	for	in	off	out	up	with
break										
bring										
carry							x			
come										
cut										
get								x		
hold										
make										
put									x	
take										
talk										

Chart of common verbs and particles

Key to Example Exercises in Chapters 5 and 6

CHAPTER 5

Pages 69, 70 (Inferring meaning from a context. Suggestions only).

1	*fossilized*	pre-historic
2	*forefinger*	thumb, crack between thumb and forefinger
3	*narrow*	only forty miles from the sea to the Swedish border
4	*splintering*	smashed by some gigantic hammer; thousands of particles.
5	*breakage*	splintering bones and knuckles into thousands of particles; this (breakage).
6	*shards*	shattered into a thousand fragments; the sea has flowered in to form a million creeks, gullies, bays and gorges.
7	*creeks*	sea has flowed in; gullies, bays and gorges; winding narrow defiles.
8	*fjords*	winding narrow defiles where the mountains fall sheer to glittering water; these (are the fjords).
9	*keel*	sailors; water.
10	*navigated*	sailed to Greenland and America; from the Mediterranean to Iceland.

Page 73 (Area of reference)
1C, 2D, 3A, 4E, 5B.

Page 73 (Level of formality)

Formal	*Neutral*	*Informal*
associate	friend	pal
	companion	mate
		buddy

Pages 73, 74 (Collocation)
hew down a tree; carve roast meat; slit open an envelope; hack at a door; carve one's initials on a tree; chop wood; carve wood; slit a skirt; hew coal; cut a finger; cut off a branch of a tree; slit one's wrist; hack at a wooden barrier.

Page 74 (Scale)

	+	++	+++
(1)	big	spacious	immense
	large	extensive	gigantic
			colossal
			enormous
(2)	little	tiny	minute
	small	diminutive	microscopic
			infinitesimal
(3)	well-known	famous	illustrious
		distinguished	renowned
(4)	hut	cottage	mansion
	cabin	house	castle
			palace
(5)	breeze	gale	hurricane
	wind	storm	

Page 75 (Specific/General) (Note: there are many possibilities here, depending on how specific/general you wish to be!

	Specific ─────────────────────→		*General*
	tulip	flower	plant
(1)	cow	cattle	animal (etc.)
(2)	coupé/limousine/ saloon	car	vehicle
(3)	chisel/hammer	tool	instrument

(4)	novel (noun)	story	book
(5)	novelist	author	writer
(6)	jeans	trousers	clothes
(7)	pineapple	fruit	food
(8)	whisky	liquor	drink
(9)	scream (noun)	cry	sound/noise
(10)	race	run	move

Page 76 (Attitude)
frugal (+), miserly (−), careful (=); famous (+), notorious (−); extravagant (−), generous (+); strict (=), severe (−); obstinate (−), resolute (+); inactive (=/−), lazy (−), tired (=), sleepy (=); bright (+), gaudy (−); self-respect (+), snobbery (−); rashness (−), courage (+); advertise (=), boast (−), brag (−).

Pages 77, 78 (Antonyms)
(1) *borrowed. (2) *nephew. (3) brilliant. (4) obey. (5) clear. (*reciprocal antonyms. *Command/obey* (4) are not reciprocal antonyms: a general may command, but his soldiers will not *necessarily* obey him!)

Pages 78, 79 (Antonyms: prefixes)
elegant–inelegant; possible–impossible; legal–illegal;
regular–irregular; convenient–inconvenient;
probable/improbable; sensitive–insensitive; moral–immoral;
literate–illiterate; relevant–irrelevant.

Pages 79, 80 (Relationships)
(1)   Jonathan is Peter's *nephew*.
(2)   Peter is Jonathan's *uncle*.
(3)   Jonathan and Bill are *brothers*.
(4)   Miriam and Jean are *cousins*.
(5)   Eileen is Peter's *mother-in-law*.

Pages 80, 81 (Display)
(a) steering wheel – 8; (b) radiator grille – 4; (c) bumper/fender – 11; (d) sidelight – 1; (e) bonnet/hood – 10; (f) indicator light – 2;

(g) wing-mirror – 5; (h) numberplate – 12; (i) windscreen wiper/ windshield wiper – 9; (j) headlight/headlamp – 3; (k) windscreen/ windshield – 6; (l) rear-view mirror – 7.

Page 81 (Hierarchies)
Capacity: gallon, quart, pint, gill, fluid ounce.
Army Organization: army, regiment, battalion, company, platoon.
Royal Navy ranks: Admiral, Commodore, Captain, Commander, Lieutenant, Petty Officer, Able Seaman.

Page 83 (Pronunciation)

/θ/	/ð/
bath	bathe
theory	then
theft	gather
through	
mathematics	

Page 84 (Grammatical information)
(1)   bought – buy; brought – bring; understood – understand; caught – catch; lay – lie.
(2)   travel – Br. travelling/US traveling; hop – hopping; brag – bragging; mail – mailing; exceed – exceeding; rob – robbing. (Briefly, the main rules for doubling of a consonant are: the final consonant is doubled when the preceding vowel is stressed and spelled with a single letter (*hop – hopping*; *prefer – preferring*); there is no doubling when the vowel is unstressed or written with two letters (*enter – entering*; *exceed – exceeding*); Br. Eng., but not Am. Eng., breaks the second rule with respect to the consonants $l \rightarrow ll$; $m \rightarrow mm$, $p \rightarrow pp$ (hence Br. *travelling*/US *traveling*). There are also some additional rules: see *A Grammar of Contemporary English*, pp. 107–108.)

CHAPTER 6

Page 87 (Prefixes)
1 – E, 2 – D, 3 – B, 4 – A, 5 – C.

Page 84 (Prefixes: meaning)
(1)   misprint: something printed *wrongly*.
(2)   mislaid: put in the *wrong* place and therefore lost.
(3)   misguided: *wrong*, incorrect.
(4)   misquoted: *wrongly* quoted.
(5)   misunderstood: *wrongly* understood.
(6)   misconduct: *bad* conduct.
(7)   mistrust: '*bad* trust', i.e. lack of trust.

Page 88 (Suffixes)
(1) classes: classified; (2) identity: identified;
(3) terror: terrified; (4) simpler: simplified; (5) just: justify.

Page 95 (Adjective + noun collocations)
1 – B calculated risk; 2 – D deliberate mistake;
3 – A voluntary retirement; 4 – E premeditated murder;
5 – C considered judgement; 6 – G express wish;
7 – F wilful ignorance. (Other collocations, e.g. wilful murder are,
of course, possible.)